Special Issue
Journal of East European Management Studies
JEEMS

Editorial Committee: Prof. Dr. Thomas Steger, Prof. Dr. Rainhart Lang, Dr. Tiia Vissak

Editorial Office: Prof. Dr. Thomas Steger, Universität Regensburg, Wirtschaftswissenschaftliche Fakultät, Lehrstuhl für BWL II, insb. Führung und Organisation, Universitätsstr. 31, 93053 Regensburg

Monika Wieczorek-Kosmala | Igor Gurkov
Thomas Steger [Eds.]

Challenges of Management in the COVID-19 Reality

Onlineversion
Nomos eLibrary

The Deutsche Nationalbibliothek lists this publication in the
Deutsche Nationalbibliografie; detailed bibliographic data
are available on the Internet at http://dnb.d-nb.de

ISBN   978-3-98542-027-8 (Print)
        978-3-95710-398-7 (ePDF)
ISSN   0949-6181

British Library Cataloguing-in-Publication Data
A catalogue record for this book is available from the British Library.

ISBN   978-3-98542-027-8 (Print)
        978-3-95710-398-7 (ePDF)
ISSN   0949-6181

Library of Congress Cataloging-in-Publication Data
Wieczorek-Kosmala, Monika | Gurkov, Igor | Steger, Thomas
Challenges of Management in the COVID-19 Reality
Monika Wieczorek-Kosmala | Igor Gurkov | Thomas Steger (Eds.)
133 pp
Includes bibliographic references.

ISBN   978-3-98542-027-8 (Print)
        978-3-95710-398-7 (ePDF)
ISSN   0949-6181

Edition Rainer Hampp in der Nomos Verlagsgesellschaft

1st Edition 2022
© Nomos Verlagsgesellschaft, Baden-Baden, Germany 2022. Overall responsibility for
manufacturing (printing and production) lies with Nomos Verlagsgesellschaft mbH & Co. KG.

This work is subject to copyright. All rights reserved. No part of this publication may be reproduced or transmitted in any form or by any means, electronic or mechanical, including photocopying, recording, or any information storage or retrieval system, without prior permission in writing from the publishers. Under § 54 of the German Copyright Law where copies are made for other than private use a fee is payable to "Verwertungsgesellschaft Wort", Munich.

No responsibility for loss caused to any individual or organization acting on or refraining from action as a result of the material in this publication can be accepted by Nomos or the editors.

Table of Contents

Editorial

Monika Wieczorek-Kosmala, Igor Gurkov, Thomas Steger
Guest Editorial 7

Articles

Robin Čejka, Tomáš Sadílek
Human resource managers in the time of COVID-19 crisis: The case of the Czech Republic 10

Almina Bešić, Christian Hirt, Zijada Rahimić
'We are quite well prepared' – Developing HR systems in response to the Covid-19 pandemic in Bosnia and Herzegovina 28

Tim Gittins, Gergely Freész, Loretta Huszák
The response of Hungarian SMEs to the Covid-19 pandemic: a Resilience Adaption Model 49

Bogna Kaźmierska-Jóźwiak, Paweł Sekuła, Błażej Socha
COVID-19 implications on the Polish stock market – the sector indices level 70

Research Notes

Krzysztof Obłój, Mariola Ciszewska-Mlinarič, Aleksandra Wąsowska, Piotr Wójcik, Tadeusz Milancej
Taming discontinuity: evolution of managerial perceptions, emotions and actions in the pandemic environment. Evidence from Poland 91

Ivan Shchetinin, Sergey Lapshin
Exploration and Exploitation of Nascent Local Business Opportunities during the Global Disruption: Strategic Actions of Subsidiaries of Large Multinational IT Corporations in Russia in the period of the COVID-19 Pandemic 107

Mane Beglaryan, Vache Gabrielyan, Gayane Shakhmuradyan
Human Resource Management during the COVID-19 Pandemic: Evidence from Armenia 120

Guest Editorial

*Monika Wieczorek-Kosmala, Igor Gurkov, Thomas Steger**

Dear readers

Since the onset of the new millennium, the world has been threatened by the occurrence of outbreaks of infectious diseases (e.g., SARS in 2008, swine flu in 2009, Ebola in 2013–2014, and Zika in 2015), igniting a discussion on whether we are prepared for the possible consequences of pandemic risk in societal and economic dimensions (Estrada et al. 2016; Woolnought and Kramer 2007). However, the consequences of the COVID-19 pandemic outbreak are unprecedented in numerous dimensions. Social-distancing restrictions, border closures, ban on mass events, and the lockdowns were implemented, leading to severe disturbances in the operating activities of numerous businesses worldwide. Despite such severe restrictions, we observe that COVID-19 continues with undefined persistence, as we are unable to predict when and where we may expect the next peaks of infections or new worrying mutations.

The emergence of the COVID-19 pandemic and the multidimensional impacts on organizational management it brings inspired us to call for papers for this special issue. In effect, the issue presents a collection of full-length articles and research notes devoted to the experience of enterprises during the first year of the COVID-19 pandemic in various East European countries (Poland, Hungary, the Czech Republic, Russia, Armenia, and Bosnia and Herzegovina). The studies cover the presentation of tendencies and trends in particular sectors (by *Kaźmierska-Jóźwiak, Sekuła,* and *Sacha*), in-depth analyses of a pair of similar subsidiaries of multinational companies (by *Shchetinin* and *Lapshin*) and of a sample of small and medium size enterprises (by *Gittins, Freész* and *Huszák*), examinations of the impact of the pandemic on the HR management of different types of enterprises in the national economy (by *Bešić* and *Rahimić* and by *Beglaryan, Gabrielyan* and *Shakhmuradyan*), the exploration of differ-

---

* *Monika Wieczorek-Kosmala*, Post-PhD, Associate Professor, College of Finance of the University of Economics in Katowice, Poland, Department of Corporate Finance and Insurance. Email: m.wieczorek-kosmala@ue.katowice.pl. Main research interests: corporate finance, capital structure decisions, risk management, risk financing and risk transfer strategies, in this corporate insurance and alternative risk financing mechanisms.
  Igor Gurkov, Distinguished University Professor, National Research University Higher School of Economics, Moscow. Email: igor_gurkov@yahoo.com. Main research interests: Industrial innovations, corporate strategies, organizational design.
  Thomas Steger, Full Professor of Leadership and Organization, University of Regensburg. Email: thomas.steger@ur.de. Main research interests: Corporate governance, board behaviour, employee ownership.

ent managers' anticipations and reactions to the crisis situation (by *Čejka* and *Sadílek* and by *Obłój, Ciszewska-Mlinarič, Wąsowska, Wójcik*, and *Milancej*).

Most of the papers are based on surveys, but a case study and an essay which used the econometric analysis of the panel financial data are also included. It is not surprising that three out of seven papers in this issue deal with the evolution of human resource management (HRM) systems and practices and another paper also examines "how discontinuity caused by the COVID-19 [pandemic] outbreak impacts upon management". Indeed, the COVID-19 pandemic posed not only the major challenge for HRM arrangements in most companies, but also a major shock for enterprise managers who experienced not only personal stress related to the business disturbances, but also fears about their own health, the health of their family members, relatives, and close friends, having to live at times through the tragedy of losing their relatives and close friends, in addition to experiencing (or having to experience) additional worries related to "those they had tamed" —employees of enterprises they managed.

Although most of the papers are empirical in nature, they can be placed within a phenomenon- driven research approach (see Hambrick 2007; Alvesson/Sandberg 2011; Schwarz/Stensaker 2014; von Krogh et al. 2012; Doh 2015; Schwarz/Stensaker 2016). A few papers accept the approach by von Krogh et al. (2012), who stated that phenomenon-based research is inherently proto-theoretic.

A careful reading of all of the papers in this issue reveals another fact that amazed at least one guest editor of this Special Issue. Although all the countries presented in the issue got through deep transformational crises of different length after the end of Communism, and at least in two countries (Bosnia and Herzegovina and Armenia) these crises where aggravated by large scale military conflicts, no mention of this experience is found in the papers written by the authors from those countries, while an independent observer might find many similarities between the situation during the COVID-19 pandemic and the situation of the early 1990s in all countries of Eastern Europe.

This may signify two things—either the younger generation of researchers from Eastern European economies consider their countries as "post-transitional economies" and the experience of the early transition is not considered valid for the description of the consequences of the COVID-19 pandemic on enterprise management, or there a "specific psychological repression" of the memories about the "bad times" taking place. In both cases, attempts were made in most papers to present the pre-pandemic situation in their countries as a period of stable or dynamic socio-economic development.

References:

Doh, J. P. 2015. From the Editor: Why we need phenomenon-based research in international business. Journal of World Business 50(4):609–611.

Estrada, R., Griffith, A., Prim, C., Sinn, J. (2016), Pandemics in a changing climate – Evolving risk and the global response, Swiss Re, Zurich, available at: https://www.swissre.com/dam/jcr:552d59b2-76c6-4626-a91a-75b0ed58927e/Pandemics_in_a_changing_climate_Full_report_FINAL.pdf

Hambrick, D. C. 2007. The field of management's devoting to theory: Too much of a good thing? Academy of Management Journal 50(6):1346–1352.

Schwarz, G. M., and I. G. Stensaker. 2014. Time to take off the theoretical straightjacket and (re)-introduce phenomenon-driven research. Journal of Applied Behavioral Science 50(4):478–501.

Schwarz, G. M., and I. G. Stensaker. 2016. Showcasing phenomenon-driven research on organizational change. Journal of Change Management 16(4):245–264.

von Krogh, G., C. Rossi-Lamastra, and S. Haefliger. 2012. Phenomenon-based research in management and organisation science: When is it rigorous and does it matter? Long Range Planning 45(4):277–298.

Woolnough, K., Kramer, S. (2007), Influenza pandemics: Time for a reality check? Swiss Re Focus Report, Zurich, available at: https://media.swissre.com/documents/influenza_pandemics_time_for_a_reality_check_en.pdf

Human resource managers in the time of COVID-19 crisis: The case of the Czech Republic*

*Robin Čejka, Tomáš Sadílek**

Abstract

Human Resources (HR) managers play a key role during the time of a COVID-19 crisis. Decisions made by the HR personnel can significantly change the course of action taken by the company management to resolve such a crisis. COVID-19 is an external natural crisis that influenced companies around the world and HR managers need to react to it. It is therefore imperative that HR professionals can control decision making as part of crisis management. This research aims to determine how HR managers react to selected situations caused by the COVID-19 crisis in the company and how the COVID-19 crises may occur in day-to-day business operations. Data were collected during the period from March to May 2020, respondents were 91 HR managers from Czech companies. The relations between the crisis management of HR managers and the participation in crisis planning, sensemaking of HR managers, the size of the organization in which they work, the age of the managers, the length of their practice in the field, and the gender of managers were determined. The result is COVID-19 increased challenges for the HR department in all their activities that could improve the efficiency and productivity of the organization.

Keywords: HRM, COVID-19 crisis, crisis management, traditional HR practices, modern HR practices, management styles
JEL Codes: H12, O15

Introduction

In the current days, the concept of crisis is primarily perceived as an economic crisis affecting the whole society. For crisis management, however, it is appropriate to perceive the crisis as a situation threatening a certain project or business entity from various forces. Research shows that uncertainty is a fundamental factor associated with the emergence of crises (Liu/Bartz/Duke 2016). The crisis is a major threat to the survival of the system while providing little time for managers to react, a poorly structured situation and a lack of resources to manage it (Lacerda 2019). The crisis is not always based on external influences outside of the company (Bowen/Freidank/Wannow/Cavallone 2018). The most typical response of a company to a crisis is the dismissal of employees, often before assessing the causes of the crisis. This will reduce the company's costs quickly and the response, therefore, seems like a sensible measure. Identifying

---

* Received: 18.09.20, Accepted: 02.08.21, 3 revisions.
** *Robin Čejka*, Assistant professor, University of Economics and Management, Prague, Human Resources Department. Email: robin.cejka@vsem.cz. Main research interests: Human Resources Management.
Tomáš Sadílek, Assistant professor, Prague University of Economics and Business, Faculty of International Relations, Department of International Business. Email: tomas.sadilek@vse.cz. Main research interests: Consumer Behaviour, Social Entrepreneurship.

and understanding the causes of a crisis over some time can then lead us to an incorrect decision (Santana/Valle/Galan 2017). Even though the dismissal of employees is implicitly dealt with as an inevitable and universal reaction to any form of crisis, it should be the least suitable solution for both sides. Traditional crisis management approaches do not provide an effective way to address the chaos that the crisis is causing (Lacerda 2019).

The bankruptcy of a company is a deterioration of the company's performance due to an excessive reduction in its internal resources, which also occurs in the event of massive redundancy. Reducing the number of employees can increase demoralization in the company or reduce the company to a completely insufficient size to fulfil its tasks and achieve its goals. Human resource management is thus an essential element for achieving a competitive advantage even in times of crisis (Santana et al. 2017). Modern technologies alone no longer represent a sustainable competitive advantage (Ochetan and Ochetan 2012). In times of crisis, the company's human resources are the element that determines the course of other events. Crisis management strives to achieve the company's readiness for various crises. Traditionally, only a financial crisis is considered a crisis, but in practice, any disruptive event caused by people, property, equipment, or the environment can adversely affect the value of a society within a company. This places high demands on human resource managers, who must be prepared for crises and plan to intervene on the impact to human resources and thus prevent disruption to the company's operations (Vardarlier 2016). COVID-19 is an example of an external natural crisis that influenced companies around the world and HR managers need to react to it. This research aims to determine how HR managers react to selected situations caused by the COVID-19 crisis in the company and how the COVID-19 crises may occur in day-to-day business operations. The article is further divided into Literature review, Materials and methods, Results, Discussion and Conclusion.

Literature review

Success in the human resources management process is achieved by organizations that manage their human resources, follow the direction of their development, recognize the importance of human resources planning and management, and harmonize the activities of the human resources department with the economic strategy. The aim is to gain a competitive advantage by using human resources as strategic resources (Ochetan/Ochetan 2012). In the following literature review, we focus on three main challenges that HR managers faced during the COVID-19 pandemic: (1) The impact of the crisis on the company (consideration of the crisis in the strategy, the involvement of employees in crisis planning, the impact of the crisis on the HRM department and the role of the HRM department during the crisis), (2) Reaction of HR managers to the crisis (reaction to panic, to the departure of employees, reaction to fluctuations, and a decrease in motivation and morale of employees), and (3) The impact of the crisis on the company's economy (expenditure on benefits, reduction of wages due to the crisis, compensation, bad reputation, false information) and the impact of the crisis on the work of managers (crisis in the management of the company, misunderstanding of employees, increase in the volume of work, dissatisfaction of employees).

COVID-19 in the Czech Republic

The COVID-19 crisis has implications not only in the economic crisis but also from social and environmental factors. According to Hudson (2020), in many European countries, the travel and hospitality sectors were the two most impacted by the COVID-19 crisis. Of course, the impact of COVID-19 has a strong geographical impact in Eastern European countries Åslund (2020). Different countries implemented various policies on how to reduce the impact of COVID-19 on their economic environment. This is very intensive in the Czech Republic because the whole economic system is influenced by this crisis. After all, this is a small open economy. During the first wave of COVID-19 in spring 2020, the downfall of Czech enterprises or their switch to the so-called emergency economic mode with an uncertain vision (as the COVID-19 pandemic is not over yet) can result in unforeseen consequences for the economy and the entire European society (Čepel/Gavurová/Dvorský/Belás 2020). By the end of May 2020, the Czech response to the COVID-19 pandemic has been recognized as a "success" following the fast introduction of strict nationwide preventive measures (Kouřil/Ferenčuhová 2020) and this was also perceived by foreign media (Anon 2020). During this first wave of COVID-19 in the Czech Republic in March 2020, no direct financial support for employees was offered even though there was a two-week-long lockdown of many services and some production companies closed their plants to reduce the potential sharing of the COVID-19. Since April 2020, the Czech government started to help Czech companies by providing a subvention programme, loans, and donations to decrease the potential company crisis. Economic sectors that were faced with lockdown in the first wave were tourism and hospitality and gastronomy. Based on the data from Eurostat (2021), this was also visible in the change of the unemployment rate in the Czech Republic that grew from 2.0 % in March 2020 to 2.4 % in May 2020 which takes the upswing of 20 % (even though the rate is still the lowest one in the European Union).

The impact of the crisis on HR managers

The global financial crisis from 2007 to 2009 provided insight into the practical functioning of companies during crises. With credit constraints, there was a surplus of working capital, which reduced companies' performance as companies were forced to use relatively expensive sources of financing. However, the negative effects of excess working capital on the company's performance persisted for up to two years (Tsuruta 2019). Vardarlier (2016) divided reactions to crisis into categories according to style, namely to "traditional practices" and "modern practices". On one hand, traditional practices describe a low level of reaction to the crisis, which focuses on taking productivity and efficiency measures, layoffs of employees, low motivation systems, taking legal and financial risks, and negative behaviour toward employees, such as threatening, mobbing and dismissing or blaming others. On the other hand, modern practices involve establishing a crisis management team, utilization of talent management to develop loyalty, focusing on training, education, professional development, and employee assistance programs, compromising with employees and communicating via various communication channels towards employees and the proper usage of social media as well as various public tools (Vardarlier 2016).

The crisis affects all sections of the company, human resources are usually affected by panic, loss of key employees and knowledge, staff turnover, lack of morale and motivation, reduced performance, increased health care costs, litigation by employees, negative reputation, misinformation, management crisis, the inability of managers to understand employee reactions, stopping recruitment, cancelling planned employee development activities (Vardarlier 2016). In response to the shortcomings of traditional approaches, new concepts (such as directives, transformation, or cognitive leadership styles) have emerged in crisis management, as commonly used management tools do not lead to the desired result in crises (Lacerda 2019). Rational allocation of human resources in times of crisis requires an understanding of the interrelationships between employees and industrial units in the organization (Aviso/Mayol/Promentilla/Santos/Tan/Ubando/Yu 2018). Employee motivation is an important element, especially in the current global competition (Ochetan/Ochetan 2012). The effects of the crisis and recession on employees most often include an increase in workload, reorganization of work, reduction of nonwage benefits, reduction of paid overtime, forced unpaid leave, or cancellation of training. These limitations are more visible in large companies (Lai/Saridakis/Blackburn/Johnstone 2016). Based on the overmentioned studies, we conclude that responsible HR managers typically stimulates the HR department employees to participate in crisis planning and react flexibly to the situation in the company (Aviso et al.; Čepel 2020; 2018; Lacerdi 2018), and we hypothesize the following:

H1:   There is a dependence between crisis management of HR managers and the participation of an HR employee in crisis planning.

HR managers during the crisis

In this paper, we are focusing on the organizational crisis. This term could be defined as *"a low-probability, high impact event that threatens the viability of the organization and is characterized by ambiguity of cause, effect, and means of resolution, as well as by a belief that decisions must be made swiftly"* (Pearson/Clair 1998, p. 60). Bundy/Pfarrer/Short/Coombs (2017) identified the following characteristics for organizational crises: (1) crises create uncertainty, disruption, and change; (2) crises are harmful or threatening; (3) crises are behavioural phenomena, meaning that the involved actors socially construct them and (4) crises are not discrete events but parts of larger processes. In an organizational crisis, the key tool of the manager is the so-called sensemaking, which is a complex process of data collection of various natures and their subsequent application in the implementation of the right decision. Weick (1995, pp. 60–61) summarizes the term of sensemaking as follows: *"Sensemaking is something that preserves plausibility and coherence, something that is reasonable and memorable, something that embodies experience and expectations, something which resonates with other people, something that can be constructed retrospectively but also can be used prospectively, something that captures both feelings and thoughts, something that allows for embellishment to fit current oddities, something that is fun to contrast. In short, what is necessary for sensemaking is a good story"*. The importance of right sensemaking is significant during the disruptive times of a company crisis when managers need to decide very quickly and correctly how to reduce potential risks and decrease the negative influence of the crisis on the companies processes and the whole business. In times of crisis, sensemaking is based on coordinated action and then cycle back to reflect on the adequacy of the presumed sharing (Weick 2020). The COVID-19 pandemic has disrupted stable business processes and created a level of still ongoing uncertainty, which undermines the sensemaking during the crisis decision-making process (Christianson/Barton 2021). Part of this process is the application of objective information, but also the emotional information and the atmosphere found in the company (Combe/Carrington 2015). Leaders' mental models are therefore considered critical to executive performance (Carrington/Combe/Mumford 2018). The emotional response of managers in times of crisis plays an important role in shaping the collective emotional state of group members. Self-confidence allows you to make risky or controversial decisions, emotional control helps to face the negative reactions of team members, a positive attitude promotes team energy, calming, concentration, openness, and transparency, creative thinking (Lacerda 2019). The success of an organization often depends on the skills and expertise of employees, so professionals play an important role in crisis management and in rebuilding businesses after a crisis (Vardarlier 2016). Strict job definitions and strict hierarchical organization and procedures in jobs with only limited rotations, encourage employees to make full use of their knowledge (Kang/Snell 2009, Asmalovskij/Sadílek/Hinčica/Mizerová 2019).

The basic tools of human resources management to address the impact of the crisis include the reorganization of the recruitment system, re-evaluation of work analysis, the creation of new reward systems and incentives, retaining talent in the organization, reviewing short-term goals to achieve long-term goals, reviewing long-term goals themselves, and allocating strategic goals in partial steps (Vardarlier 2016). Awareness contributes to well-structured crisis management and acts as a prevention to panic crisis management (Amalou-Döpke/Süß 2014). A contingency plan should be drawn up for each organization, regardless of its type and size (Vardarlier 2016). An effective leadership style in times of crisis involves the active involvement of team members and seeks their views and suggestions for solving problems. Continuous communication efforts and encouraging team members lead to achieving the organization's vision and increase the level of interpersonal trust among business members (Lacerda 2019).

H2: *There is a dependence between crisis management of HR managers and the sensemaking of HR managers.*

Influence of company size and industry

The size of the company influences the global and systematic way of perceiving problems in the field of human resources management. Cooperation between management and employees to achieve a joint business project is an essential element of crisis survival (Ochetan/Ochetan 2012). The recession in 2008 and 2009 helped to describe the differences in the effects of the crisis on companies of different sizes. The impact on small and medium-sized enterprises was more significant than on large enterprises. Small companies focused on reducing costs, while large organizations took alternative personnel measures. Large companies lay off employees more than small and medium-sized enterprises. Small companies prefer informality in human resource management practice. However, companies with formal personnel procedures have shown greater resilience to the effects of recession (Lai et al. 2016). The decline occurs mainly when the size of the industry shrinks. There is a reduction in performance and there is a risk of its complete disappearance, as in the case of cigar production or shipbuilding (Santana et al. 2017). While job vacancies will be limited, they should focus on professionals who will contribute to the use of existing resources and capabilities (Díaz-Fernández/Pasamar-Reyes/Valle-Cabrera 2017). The situation in the environment of the Czech Republic can be assessed according to modern global trends. Human resources in the Czech environment have changed their role from a supporting element to a strategic one (Dubravská/Solanková 2015). Therefore, we hypothesize that:

H3: *There is a dependence between crisis management by HR managers and the size of the organization in which they work.*

Finally, there is the influence in the field of business and the age and length of practice of HR managers. The field of business influences how flexibly can manage reactions to crises in various fields because there are more stable fields such as companies who are doing their business in the primary sector (such as mining), heavy machinery or stable state-owned companies. More flexibility is allowed for companies such as start-ups or agile companies doing their business in the area of services (Čepel et al. 2020). The age and length of practice of HR managers vary with the growing age and length of practice of HR managers, but overall they are more experienced and can react better to crises (Wegmann/Schärrer 2020). It is not known what style HR managers deal with the impact of crises, whether their style differs depending on the field in which they work or depending on their age, length of practice, or gender (Yahya/Faozi/Al-Swidi 2021). Therefore, we hypothesize that:

H4: *There is a dependence between crisis management by HR managers and the age of managers.*

H5: *There is a dependence between the crisis management of HR managers and the length of their practice in the field.*

H6: *There is a dependence between crisis management by HR managers and the gender of managers.*

Materials and methods

Participants and procedures

The research seeks to determine the reactions of HR managers to selected situations caused by the COVID-19 crisis in companies of various sectors in the Czech Republic. Therefore, we set hypotheses on the relationship between crisis management style and sensemaking of HR managers and the participation of an HR employee in crisis planning, and the consequences of the COVID-19 crisis in the company's organization size, the age of managers, the length of their practice in the field, and the gender of managers. Data were collected during the period from March to May 2020 through the first way of COVID-19 pandemic, and the CAWI (Computer Assisted Web Interviewing) method, questioned utilizing an interactive web form, which was chosen as the research method. This method was chosen because it offered the opportunity for the rapid compilation of data and was less financially demanding compared to the collection of data in the field. The technique of convenience sampling was used to contact 185 respondents by email with a request to complete an anonymous survey and 91 of them answered. The survey was conducted among the managers of human resources departments working in companies of various sizes and various fields of business in the Czech Republic. Respondents came from all age categories with different lengths of practice in the field. When selecting potential candidates for this survey, we wanted to cover different kinds of sectors to have answers from companies that were affected by the COVID-19 crisis. This is the reason we did not focus only on the most affected sectors, such as travel services, hospitality, and gastronomy and catering.

Variables

The first part of the questionnaire deals with personnel strategy and policy in the company. These are questions 1–8, which concern the impact of the crisis on the company and HRM's response to the crisis. The second part presents scenarios that may occur as a result of the crisis and finds out the reactions of respondents to the described situations (scenarios). These are questions 9–17, which relate to the impact of the crisis on the company's economy and HRM and the crisis on the work of HR managers. The third part is compiled to classify respondents according to the defined criteria. The interviewed scenarios were created based on an overview of practices in the field of human resources compiled by Vardarlier (2016). Based on a thorough search of resources, the authors prepared an inventory of the effects of the crisis on employees and companies and defined the usual reactions of human resources staff. The questionnaire survey verifies the validity of the presented facts, examines their transferability to the Czech environment, and at the same time allows HR managers in the environment of the Czech Republic to know the style of solving situations. The situation and impacts are reformulated for the questionnaire survey, but they strive to preserve the meaning and content originally intended by the author.

One answer to each of the crisis scenario questions is defined following the traditional management style and one answer following the modern management style. It is not possible to state unequivocally that a certain defined procedure and style of the solution are correct and the only possible one. Respondents are therefore allowed to enter their way of solving situations by filling in the "Other" option. To evaluate the questionnaire and answer the hypotheses, the newly written answers were assigned to the modern or traditional style of crisis evaluation according to their content. If the answer completely deviated from both categories, it would be classified as "alternative".

SPSS software was used for the statistical testing of hypotheses. The processing of the values obtained by the questionnaire survey was started by describing the basic data set. Only qualitative variables appear throughout the survey. Survey hypotheses require a survey of the dependencies of variables. Data from the questionnaire did not come from normal classification, which was verified using the Shapiro-Wilk test. Furthermore, the data is ordinal, which is why nonparametric tests must be used to verify statistically significant differences. Therefore, in this step, we proceeded first with the chi-squared test to confirm the set hypotheses, and then Spearman's rank correlation coefficient, and Somer's D to evaluate how strong are the relations between variables in the hypotheses. The data sample obtained from 91 respondents was divided according to two features. Character 1 is the characteristics of respondents and companies, character 2 are groups of respondents according to the style of risk management in the field of HR. These groups have been created based on the second part of the questionnaire ("Response to the effects of the crisis"), which used scenarios to examine which category in the style of crisis management the respondent belongs to.

Results

A total of 91 respondents took part in the survey. None of the respondents used the opportunity to comment on the survey questionnaire or make any comments.

Respondents' characteristics

The majority of the respondents are women (58 %). The research sample is not evenly distributed among companies in different fields, business sectors are represented only in units. Respondents from subjects focused on the food industry (16.4 %), safety services (16.4 %), and the energy sector (14.2 %) predominate. The most numerous age group of respondents in the category of 36–50 years (45 %). The most represented are respondents with more than 10 years of experience (47.3 %), respondents with an experience of 0–1 years (4.4 %), even respondents with an experience of 4–5 (15.4 %) and 6–10 years (15.4 %). Among the enterprises of the respondents, medium-sized enterprises (31.5 %), micro-enterprises (24.4 %), small enterprises (22.6 %), and large enterprises (21.5 %) are the most represented. Both men and women are represented in the individual age categories. Both men and women predominate in the category of 36–50 years (50 % and 41.5 %, respectively). Even according to the length of practice, respondents with experience of over 10 years predominate in both genders (57.9 % for men and 39.6 % for women). All statistics were tested by t-test at the significance level of 0.05. Detailed information about the sample of respondents is presented in Table 1.

Table 1. Structure of respondents (n = 91)

Age of managers		The field of business of the entity in which you are currently working	
18–25	14.3 %	Safety	16.7 %
26–35	20.9 %	Food industry	16.7 %
36–50	45.1 %	Energy	14.4 %
51–65	19.8 %	Transport	8.9 %
Length of experience in the field of human resources (include positions of all levels in all enterprises for the entire career)		Education	8.9 %
0–1	4.4 %	Tourism / leisure	6.7 %
2–3	17.6 %	Construction	6.7 %
4–5	15.4 %	Finance	3.3 %
6–10	15.4 %	Ecology	2.2 %
More than 10	47.3 %	Craft activities	2.2 %
Please select the size of the enterprise you are currently working in		Agriculture	2.2 %
Microenterprise	24.4 %	Automotive	1.1 %
Small enterprise	22.6 %	Transportation, Construction	1.1 %
Medium enterprise	31.5 %	Mining activity	1.1 %
Large enterprise	21.5 %	IT	1.1 %
Gender		Metrology, testing and technical standardization	1.1 %
Male	41.8 %	Personnel agency – human resources	1.1 %
Female	58.3 %	Lawyer services	1.1 %
		Recruitment	1.1 %
		Services	1.1 %
		Textile production, trade	1.1 %

Respondents' reactions to crisis

Respondents answered a total of 13 questions, which served to identify their managerial style. If the respondent answered 7 or more questions in a style corresponding to the given category, he or she was assigned to it. If the respondent does not have a dominant style, then the answers following a certain style do not reach the number of 7 or more, it is classified into a group according to the predominant answers, considering the content of the listed answers. Other answers in the examined sample were not formed by progressive solutions, but almost exclusively by transferring the obligations to decide in each situation to the management of the company or another manager. It is, therefore, necessary to consider them not as innovative, but rather following traditional practices. No respondents were found in the file with answers that could not be assigned to a modern or traditional style due to their content, and therefore there is no "alternative" category. Following the traditional management style, a total of 66 % of respondents answered, and following the modern style, a total of 34 % of respondents. Table 2 lists the individual values obtained by the tests performed. The interpretation of the results follows below. Next, in this step, we proceeded with the chi-squared test, Spearman's rank correlation coefficients, and Somer's D.

Table 2. Results of the testing of hypotheses

	Pearson Chi-square	Spearman's ρ	Somers' D
H1: There is a dependence between crisis management of HR managers and the participation of an HR employee in crisis planning.	42.05	.67**	.63*
H2: There is a dependence between crisis management of HR managers and the sensemaking of HR managers.	25.96	.47**	.43*
H3: There is a dependence between crisis management by HR managers and the size of the organization in which they work.	24.93	.51**	.43*
H4: There is a dependence between crisis management by HR managers and the age of managers.	20.19	.46*	.41*
H5: There is a dependence between the crisis management of HR managers and the length of their practice in the field.	35.03	.56**	.51*
H6: There is a dependence between crisis management by HR managers and the gender of managers.	.63	.007	.007

Notes: *p < 0.05; **p < 0.01

As we can see from Table 2, only hypothesis H4 about the dependence between crisis management by HR managers and the gender of managers was rejected due to no significance (0.63 χ^2; 0.07 ρ; 0.07 d). The rest of the hypotheses were confirmed at the significance level p < 0.05 or p < 0.01, respectively.

Therefore, we can see positive relations between crisis management of HR managers and the age of managers (20.19 χ^2; 0.46 ρ; 0.41 d), the length of their practice in the field (35.03 χ^2; 0.56 ρ; 0.51 d), the size of the organization in which they work (24.93 χ^2; 0.51 ρ; 0.43 d). There is also a statistically significant positive relation between crisis management of HR managers and the participation of an HR employee in crisis planning (42.05 χ^2; 0.67 ρ; 0.63 d) and sensemaking of HR managers (25.96 χ^2; 0.47 ρ; 0.43 d). The survey showed that especially HR managers of micro and small enterprises believe that the impact of the crisis on the strategic role of human resources in the company does not fall at all (Table 3). However, HR managers in large companies confirm, in line with the findings of current studies, that the crisis strengthens the strategic role of human resources in the organization.

Table 3. Respondents' views on the strategic role of management based on the enterprise size

Enterprise size	No influence	Weaken	Strengthen	Total
Microenterprise	23.1 %	4.4 %	4.4 %	31.9 %
Small enterprise	9.9 %	2.2 %	13.2 %	25.3 %
Medium enterprise	0.0 %	2.2 %	23.1 %	25.3 %
Large enterprise	0.0 %	2.2 %	15.4 %	17.6 %
Total	32.9 %	10.9 %	56.1 %	100.0 %

A total of 25.6 % of respondents expressed the opinion that the human resources department never plays a vital role in crisis management. Respondents who are aware of the importance of the role of HR management before, during, and after the crisis come mainly from large and medium-sized enterprises. This can also be seen in Table 4.

Table 4. Opinions of managers on the importance of the HR department in crisis management

When does the HR department play a crucial role in crisis management?	Microenterprise	Small enterprise	Medium enterprise	Large enterprise	Total
During the crisis	7.78 %	10.0 %	11.1 %	2.2 %	31.1 %
During the crisis, After the crisis	0.0 %	2.2 %	1.1 %	1.1 %	4.4 %
Never	18.9 %	6.7 %	0.0 %	0.0 %	25.6 %
After the crisis	1.1 %	2.2 %	0.0 %	0.0 %	3.3 %
Before the crisis	2.2 %	0.0 %	0.0 %	3.3 %	5.6 %
Before the crisis, During the crisis	0.0 %	3.33 %	3.33 %	1.1 %	7.78 %
Before the crisis, During the crisis, After the crisis	2.2 %	1.1 %	8.9 %	8.9 %	21.1 %
Before the crisis, After the crisis	0.0 %	0.0 %	1.1 %	0.0 %	1.1 %
Total	32.2 %	25.6 %	25.6 %	16.7 %	100.0 %

Discussion

The research on the exploration of the reactions of HR managers to selected situations caused by the COVID-19 crisis in companies of various sectors in the Czech Republic was conducted from March to May 2020 with a sample of 91 respondents. The relations between the crisis management of HR managers and the participation of an HR employee in crisis planning, sensemaking of HR managers, the size of the organization in which they work, the age of the managers, the length of their practice in the field, and the gender of managers were determined. Based on the previous studies, the situation in the environment of the Czech Republic can be assessed according to global trends, therefore the findings from the research of Vardarlier (2016) were used to determine the styles of crisis management by human resources managers. The comparison of reactions of HR managers towards the crisis is quite limited because the CRANET surveys from 2017 do not include the Czech Republic in its survey CRANET 2017) and in 2011 respondents from the Czech Republic demonstrated a very low response rate (just 54 responses) and this research was partially focused on the influence of the financial crisis in 2008–2009 where they only commented on decreasing number of employees due to this crisis (CRANET 2011). The respondents did not ask any additional questions or comment on the survey and it can be considered that the questions were comprehensible. Previous research (Aviso et al. 2018; Lacerdi 2018) found that human resource management is one of the essential tools for preventing a crisis in all its phases and the existence of crisis planning at the level of human resource management is key to achieving a result with the least possible loss of business. That was confirmed by hypothesis H1 that there exists a statistically significant positive dependence between crisis management of HR managers and the participation of an HR employee in crisis planning. Positive relations between crisis management of HR managers and the age of managers, sensemaking of HR managers, the length of their practice in the field, and the size of the organization in which they work were confirmed by hypotheses H2–H6 what is in line with studies of (Ahmed/Khan/Thitivesa/Siraphatthada/Phumdara 2020, Amalou-Döpke/Süß 2014, Čepel et al. 2020, Díaz-Fernández et al. 2017, and Yahya/Faozi/Al-Swidi 2021). This study showed that especially HR managers of small businesses and microenterprises believe that the impact of the crisis on the strategic role of human resources in the company does not fall at all. However, HR managers in large companies confirm, in line with the findings of (Santana et al. 2017), that crisis strengthens the strategic role of human resources in the organization. Crisis management is an effort by a company to avert a crisis before statutes related to crisis management also need to be defined and updated before, during, and after the crisis. In all these phases, human resources play a crucial role. However, a surprisingly high number of HR managers (a total of 25.6 %) expressed the view that the human resources department never plays a key role in crisis management. Additionally, HR managers with longer experience declared that they can better react to the crisis because they already overcame some company crises in the past and know better how to react. Respondents who are aware of the importance of the role of HR management before, during, and after the crisis come exclusively from large and medium-sized enterprises.

Moreover, in line with (Čepel et al. 2020), the most negatively affected industries are services (including travel, hospitality, and some non-food retail stores that were not allowed to be opened) and selected manufacturing, which is stagnating. Some companies had to stop their production for some time due to COVID-19 restrictions or problems with the supply of raw materials and semi-products mostly from Asian countries as well as complications with enough employees from abroad who rather decided to stay in their home countries. Therefore, the perception of the crisis varies by different sectors significantly because the food and pharmaceuticals industries were minimally affected by the crisis and some entrepreneurs tried to use the situation for new business opportunities. The crisis is characterized by its unpredictability and it is therefore not possible to decide unequivocally whether the traditional approach to crisis management is always inappropriate and modern. A recommendation for further research is to complement existing quantitative research with a qualitative one that can identify those progressive HR approaches that can help alleviate the crisis. Nevertheless, a search of expert sources (such as Ahmed et al. 2020, Bennet/McWhorter 2021, Carnevale/Hatak 2020, Caligiuri/De Cieri/Minbaeva/Verbeke/Zimmermann 2020, Čepel et al. 2020, Wegmann/Schäarrer 2020) shows that modern approaches to crisis management show better results in preventing further organic development of the Covid-19 crisis in the company.

Limitations

However, a survey conducted on a sample of 91 respondents showed that traditional approaches to solving crises prevail in the Czech environment. A total of 66 % of respondents would respond to the presented crisis scenarios traditionally. Unfortunately, the relationship between management style and the field of business could not be proven due to the lack of data. Another limitation is also the nature of the data because there are only nominal and ordinal variables that enable to do only analysis by associations and not to proceed with regression analysis or structural equations modelling. Although the contingency tables suggest that coherence may exist, many sectors in this survey are represented by only one respondent. An interesting finding, which also requires an extension of the sample of respondents to confirm, pointed to a possible relationship between the style of crisis management by HR managers and the age of these managers. In the examined sample, the number of respondents with the traditional approach strongly outweighs the number of respondents with a modern approach to management in the category of 18–35 years. The relationship in the researched sample was found between the style of crisis management by HR managers and the length of their practice in the field. The number of respondents with a traditional approach in the group with 2–5 years of experience strongly outweighs the number of respondents with a modern approach. Whether this phenomenon can be attributed to a certain caution of a beginning worker, the influence of teaching at universities, or another cause could be demonstrated by further investigation through guided interviews. The survey shows that there is no significant difference between the approach to crisis management by women and men, thus the psychological characteristics of men and women do not apply. It would be appropriate to further investigate the relationship between the style of crisis management by HR managers and the size of the organization in which they work. In large companies, 100 % of respondents with a modern style were recorded. When filling in responses to individual crisis scenarios, respondents often limited themselves to listing that solving the situation is the task of the company's management. In this article, we focused only on the quantitative survey on how managers can adapt to the organizational crisis influenced by COVID-19. To do in-depth interviews to determine managers' motivation is a very good idea for the next research.

Implications for theory

Deriving findings from data collected during the current COVID-19 crisis contributes to the existing literature on performance and decision-making theory on crisis management in the HR field. The sample of Czech managers can provide initial insight on how the current COVID-19 pandemics influenced crisis management in Central and East Europe. It can be also perceived as a credible starting point to refine an academic understanding of how COVID-19 is tackled by organisational crises. Further researches with more participants, in-depth interviews, and other studies using qualitative methods should contribute in future. This study can also widen the current state of the art in crisis management influenced by the COVID-19 pandemic in Central and East Europe (Carnevale/ Hatak2020; Čepel et al. 2020).

Practical implications

The findings of researchers show that there should be no fundamental changes in the company outside the consciousness of management. However, this fact does not limit the human resources manager's activities in crisis management. Thanks to its expertise, it is equipped with the experience and knowledge necessary to decide how to respond optimally to situations. At the same time, success in the process of human resource management is achieved by organizations that involve their employees. COVID-19 influences negatively global economies and markets, but at the same time it also brings different opportunities for organizations and it is based on their management systems and flexibility, how to adapt to a new situation.

The COVID-19 increased challenges for the HR department in all their activities that could improve the efficiency and productivity of the organization. Therefore, one of the biggest challenges for HR managers during COVID-19 is how to engage employees effectively and to improve running processes in the organization.

The long-term implications of COVID-19 are currently unknown, there is little reason to believe its impact on companies and employees will be short-lived (Carnevale/Hatak 2020), even more, the changes in the Czech economy go slower than in other European economies. Furthermore, as health experts have cautioned, not only are the effects of the current pandemic far from over (Hixon 2020) but the risk of future health crises of this far-reaching nature is almost guaranteed (Desmond-Hellmann 2020).

Conclusion

The situation of the research sample corresponds to the findings of previous studies as the traditional style of crisis management by HR managers predominates in the group of respondents. The approach of HR managers to crises is influenced by the size of the company in which the respondent works. Managers of large companies are more often aware of the importance of human resources in solving the crisis and at the same time apply modern management approaches rather than managers of micro and small enterprises. The age of managers, the length of their practice in the field, the size of the organization in which they work, and the sensemaking of HR managers have a demonstrable effect on management style. The results show that the older age of the respondents and the longer length of practice was combined with the modern style of crisis management.

References

Ahmed, T., Khan, M. S., Thitivesa, D., Siraphatthada, Y., and Phumdara, T. (2020): Impact of Employees Engagement and Knowledge Sharing on Organizational Performance: Study of HR Challenges in COVID-19 Pandemic. Human Systems Management. 39, 4, 589–601.

Amalou-Döpke, L., and Süß, S. (2014): HR Measurement as an Instrument of the HR Department in Its Exchange Relationship with Top Management: A Qualitative Study Based on Resource Dependence Theory. Scandinavian Journal of Management. 30, 4, 444–460.

Anon. (2020): Slovakia Earns Reputation as a Success Story in the Coronavirus Pandemic. The Slovak Spectator. Retrieved January 28, 2020, from https://spectator.sme.sk/c/22404507/slovakia-earnsreputation-as-a-success-story-in-the-coronavirus-pandemic.html.

Åslund. A. (2020): Responses to the COVID-19 crisis in Russia, Ukraine, and Belarus. Eurasian Geography and Economics, 1–14.

Asmalovskij, A., Sadílek, T., Hinčica, V., and Mizerová, M. (2019): Performance of Social Enterprises in the Czech Republic. Journal of Social Entrepreneurship, 10, 1, 1–11.

Aviso, K. B., Mayol, A. P., Promentilla, M. A. B., Santos, J. R., Tan, R. R., Ubando, A. T., and Yu, K. D. (2018): Allocating Human Resources in Organizations Operating under Crisis Conditions: A Fuzzy Input-output Optimization Modeling Framework. Resources, Conservation and Recycling. 128, 250–258.

Bennet, E. E. and McWhorter, R. M. (2021): Virtual HRD's Role in Crisis and the Post Covid-19 Professional Lifeworld: Accelerating Skills for Digital Transformation. Advances in Developing Human Resources. 23, 1, 5–25.

Bowen, M., Freidank, J., Wannow, S., and Cavallone, M. (2017): Effect of Perceived Crisis Response on Consumers' Behavioral Intentions During a Company Scandal–An Intercultural Perspective. Journal of International Management. 24, 3, 222–237.

Bundy, J., Pfarrer, M.D., Short, C.E., and Coombs, W.T. (2017): Crises and crisis management: integration, interpretation, and research development. Journal of Management. 43, 6, 1661–1692.

Caligiuri, P., De Cieri, H., Minbaeva, D., Verbeke, A., and Zimmermann, A. (2020): International HRM insights for navigating the COVID-19 pandemic: Implications for future research and practice. Journal of International Business Studies. 51, 697–713

Carnevale, J. B., and Hatak, I. (2020): Employee Adjustment and Well-Being in the Era of COVID-19: Implications for Human Resource Management. Journal of Business Research. 116, 183–187.

Carrington, D. J., Combe, I. A., and Mumford, M. D. (2018): Cognitive Shifts Within Leader and Follower Teams: Where Consensus Develops in Mental Models During an Organizational Crisis. The Leadership Quarterly. 30, 3, 335–350.

CRANET (2011): Survey on Comparative Human Resource Management: International Executive Report 2011.

CRANET (2017): Survey on Comparative Human Resource Management: International Executive Report 2017.

Čepel, M., Gavurová, B., Dvorský, J., and Belás, J. (2020): The impact of the COVID-19 crisis on the perception of business risk in the SME segment. Journal of International Studies. 13, 3, 248–263.

Christianson, M. K., and Barton, M. A. (2021): Sensemaking in the Time of COVID-19. Journal of Management Studies. 58, 2, 572–576.

Combe, I. A, and Carrington, D. J. (2015): Leaders' Sensemaking Under Crises: Emerging Cognitive Consensus Over Time Within Management Teams. The Leadership Quarterly. 26, 3, 307–322.

Desmond-Hellmann, S. (2020): Preparing for the Next Pandemic. Retrieved April 17, 2020, from https://www.wsj.com/articles/preparing-for-the-next-pandemic-11585936915.

Díaz-Fernández, M., Pasamar-Reyes, S., and Valle-Cabrera, R. (2017): Human Capital and Human Resource Management to Achieve Ambidextrous Learning: A Structural Perspective. BRQ Business Research Quarterly. 20, 1, 63–77.

Dubravska, M, and Solankova, E. (2015): Recent Trends in Human Resources Management in Selected Industry in Slovakia and The Czech Republic. Procedia Economics and Finance. 26 1014–1019.

Hixon, T. (2020): Get Ready To Live With COVID-19. Retrieved January 31, 2021, from https://www.forbes.com/sites/toddhixon/2020/03/12/get-ready-to-live-with-covid-19/#26f55d347824.

Eurostat. (2021): Unemployment by sex and age – monthly data. Retrieved January 31, 2021, from https://ec.europa.eu/eurostat/databrowser/view/une_rt_m/default/table?lang=en

Hudson, D. S. (2020): Chapter 5. The economic, social and environmental impacts of COVID 19. In: Hudson, D.S. (ed). Oxford: Goodfellow Publishers

Kang, S., and Snell, S. A. (2009): Intellectual Capital Architectures and Ambidextrous Learning: a Framework for Human Resource Management. Journal of Management Studies. 46, 1, 65–92.

Lacerda, T. C. (2019): Crisis Leadership in Economic Recession: A Three-barrier Approach to Offset External Constraints. Business Horizons. 62, 2, 185–197.

Lai, Y., Saridakis, G., Blackburn, R. A., and Johnstone, S. (2016): Are the HR Responses of Small Firms Different from Large Firms in Times of Recession? Journal of Business Venturing, 31, 1, 113–131.

Liu, B. F., Bartz, L., and Duke, N. (2016): Communicating crisis uncertainty: A review of the knowledge gaps. Public Relations Review, 42, 3, 479–487.

Kouřil, P., and Ferenčuhová, S. (2020): "Smart" quarantine and "blanket" quarantine: the Czech response to the COVID-19 pandemic. Eurasian Geography and Economics. 1–11.

Ochetan, C. M. T., and Ochetan, D. A. (2012): The Influence of Economic and Financial Crisis on Human Resources Management. Procedia Economics and Finance. 3, 769–774.

Pearson, C.M. and Clair, J.A. (1998). Reframing crisis management. Academy of Management Review. 23, 1, 59–76.

Santana, M., Valle, R., and Galan, J.-L. (2017): Turnaround strategies for companies in crisis: Watch out the causes of decline before firing people. BRQ Business Research Quarterly. 20, 3, 206–211.

Tsuruta, D. (2019): Working Capital Management During the Global Financial Crisis: Evidence from Japan. Japan and the World Economy. 49, 206–219.

Yahya, M. H. H., Faozi A. A., and Al-Swidi, A. (2021): Factors Influencing Crisis Management: A systematic review and synthesis for future research, Cogent Business & Management, 8, 1–45.

Vardarlier, P. (2016): Strategic Approach to Human Resources Management During Crisis. Procedia-Social and Behavioral Sciences. 235, 463–472.

Weick, K. E. (1995): Sensemaking in Organizations. Thousand Oaks, CA: Sage Publications.

Weick, K. E. (2020): Sensemaking, Organizing, and Surpassing: A Handoff. Journal of Management Studies, 1–12.

Wegmann, R. M. and Schärrer, L. (2020): Outpacing the pandemic? A factorial survey on decision speed of COVID-19 task forces. Journal of Organizational Effectiveness: People and Performance, 7, 2, 191–202.

'We are quite well prepared' – Developing HR systems in response to the Covid-19 pandemic in Bosnia and Herzegovina[*]

Almina Bešić, Christian Hirt, Zijada Rahimić[**]

Abstract

The Covid-19 pandemic has caused a worldwide crisis and profoundly affected businesses. Since governmental support is limited, companies in transition economies are particularly vulnerable to crises. In our study, we address the question of how companies from the banking sector in the transition economy of Bosnia and Herzegovina utilise their HR practices to deal with the repercussions of the Covid-19 pandemic. Postulating the need for a strategic approach, we assume that HR systems can help banks to face the challenge: sink or swim through the pandemic. Based on strategic human resource and crisis management, we exploit group interviews with six banks to identify HR practice bundles. Contrary to traditional crisis management, we identify HR practices which aim at stabilising instead of downsizing in order to survive. Our findings show a positive development in Bosnian banks towards a more strategic HR; however, with only rudimentary HR practice bundles which focus on employee engagement, strengthening company culture and digitalisation to achieve a horizontal fit. We discuss implications for HR practitioners and suggest actionable principles to help HR managers respond to future crises. Future research can benefit from further exploring horizontal HR practice fit in a dynamic environment.

Keywords: HR system, horizontal fit, stabilisation, digitalisation, Bosnia and Herzegovina, banking sector, Covid-19
JEL Codes: J24; M5; O15

Introduction

The Covid-19 pandemic has profoundly affected societies worldwide. At the time of writing, the global death toll of the pandemic had exceeded 3.9 million (Johns Hopkins University 2021). Governmental measures – (partial) lockdowns, restrictions of movement, and the closure of non-essential venues – have impacted economies across the globe. This has forced many businesses to change strategies (Wenzel et al. 2021) and business models (Ritter/Pedersen

---

[*] Received: 27.12.20, Accepted: 3.9.21, 1 revision
[**] *Almina Bešić*, Dr., Assistant Professor, Johannes Kepler University Linz, Department of International Management. Email: almina.besic@jku.at. Main research interests: International human resource management, employment of migrant workers, new forms of work, gender and diversity management.
Christian Hirt, Dr., Senior Lecturer, University of Graz, Department of Human Resource Management. Email: christian.hirt@uni-graz.at. Main research interests: International human resource management, cross-cultural management.
Zijada Rahimić, Dr., Professor, School of Economics and Business University of Sarajevo, Department of Management and Organization. Email: zijada.rahimic@efsa.unsa.ba. Main research interests: Strategic human resource management, gender and diversity management.

2020). Crisis management, as an important tool for survival, can help businesses make decisions regarding the postponement of strategic investments or the restructuring of their workforce. In addition, support with furlough schemes and support payments can keep companies afloat, but these cause radical changes in human resource management (HRM). For example, the new emphasis on remote work caused by the pandemic has catapulted HRM from a peripheral to a crucial position in the new world of work (Carnevale/Hatak 2020). This certainly affects the set of human resource (HR) practices applied in organisations.

Governments in transition economies have struggled to effectively manage the pandemic. While governmental support has been crucial for many organisations, some sectors are not eligible. In such cases, it has been up to companies themselves to take remedial actions and decide on effective HR practice bundles independent of governmental support but suitable for manoeuvring through the pandemic. In our contribution, we question, whether the Covid-19 pandemic as one of the most dramatic events in recent history (Trougakos et al. 2020; Diebold 2020) can be a trigger for a more strategic approach in HRM. We analyse this by investigating HR practices of companies in the banking sector in Bosnia and Herzegovina (henceforth: Bosnia), a transition economy in South-Eastern Europe (SEE). Bosnia is an interesting context as it has a very complex institutional environment (see also Ortlieb et al. 2019), where the Covid-19 pandemic has been a major challenge for the economy.

The case of the Bosnian banking sector is interesting for two major reasons. First, it includes domestic as well as internationally owned companies with differing HR practices and overall strategic approaches to HRM (see e.g. Bešić/Ortlieb 2019; Bešić/Hirt 2016). Second, although the sector is important for the economic development of a country, it is also volatile to crises due to a lack of governmental support. Thus, our main research question reads: *How do companies in the banking sector in Bosnia respond to the changes in business operations resulting from the Covid-19 pandemic through their HR practices?*

This study contributes to the literature in two ways. First, we shed light on how companies can help themselves in a crisis when access to governmental support is not available or limited.[1] The challenges faced by organisations create a need for adapting HR practices to cope with this new environment. Second, we address the theory-practice gap (e.g. Wright/McMahan 1992; Cohen 2007; DeNisi et al. 2014) and highlight that researchers generally fail to provide 'actionable and value-added managerial principles' as criticised by Kaufman (2012). There is a need to provide specific suggestions on what companies can do to add value to their HR work. Already Elinor Ostrom (1990) showed the importance of underlying principles and that self-administration often works better than market

1 Given the fact that the Covid-19 pandemic has caused a global crisis, the terms "Covid-19 pandemic" and "crisis" will henceforth be used synonymously.

or state governance. Drawing on this idea, companies will have to organise themselves and self-determine their relevant resources for survival. Although there is no one recipe for all (Ostrom 1990), we provide theoretical guidance on choosing HR practices in a particular sector of a transition economy in order to master the crisis resulting from the Covid-19 pandemic. Furthermore, we show for the banking sector that digitally supported HR practices aiming at stabilisation are more important than pure downsizing.

In the following, we first elaborate on the relevant literature on HR in transition economies before outlining the context of Bosnia. We then explain our qualitative methodology and present our findings. We conclude with a discussion, implications for theory and practice, limitations and highlight avenues for future research.

Literature review

In many transition economies, the HR function is rather operative with little strategic focus (Bešić/Ortlieb 2019; Vuk 2012), which poses severe challenges for a new normal at the workplace. In this context, experimenting with best practices seems to be the prevalent tool for managing people. Best practices, however, are easily imitable. Since their focus lies on achieving a competitive advantage, they are not solely adequate to cope with a crisis. Furthermore, the concept of best practices as suggested by Pfeffer (1994) is contested in the European context. Best practices, such as performance-based compensation or job security, are widespread in European companies and can no longer help provide competitiveness (Lebrenz 2020). In challenging times of a pandemic, companies pre-eminently struggle with survival and seem to foreground practices such as wage cuts and lay-offs. The need for companies to take strategies into consideration remains unchanged, but the focus of reasoning for the deployment of HR practices has shifted from primarily achieving a long-term competitive advantage to managing long-term survival. Hence, there is strong need to rethink HR activities.

Learning is the key factor for survival (Gold/Smith 2003), and experience from previous crises can result in a combination of HR practices that can help master future human resource challenges. Drawing on the resource-based view (Barney/Wright 1998; Wright et al. 2001) and the concept of horizontal fit in strategic human resource management (Schuler/Jackson 1987; Boxall/Purcell 2016), we argue that companies which succeed in managing a bundle of HR practices will be able to cope with the challenges of the Covid-19 pandemic. Two research strands are interesting in this regard: strategic human resource management research on HR systems and research on crisis management.

Strategic human resource management literature either focuses on the alignment of a strategy with the human capital pool (e.g. Wright et al. 1994) or HR practices (e.g. Lado/Wilson 1994) to predominately explain a competitive advantage. Whereas both streams emphasise that one single HR practice is easily imitable, Lado and Wilson (1994) argue that companies will have to focus on HR systems. Following this train of thought, several best practice systems were suggested (e.g. Arthur 1994). Surprisingly, there is not one single best practice consistently represented in all of these systems. Tying in with Kaufman's (2012) criticism, which addresses the need for managerial guidelines, this underscores how research fails to prescribe specific choices of HR practices in specific situations. Strategic human resource management further emphasises integration and adaptation (Schuler 1992). In developing an HR strategy aligned with the business strategy, companies must increasingly consider context and configuration. This enables them to bundle specific HR practices according to their specific business environment. In times of a pandemic, combining HR practices to achieve an internal horizontal fit is considered more helpful than the application of single random HR practices.

Crisis management literature sheds light on how companies respond to crises, including the Covid-19 pandemic. Wenzel et al. (2021) give an overview of four strategic responses identified in literature which can provide answers for companies to master the Covid-19 pandemic. *Retrenchment* narrows the scope of a company's business activities by, for example, cutting costs. Although necessary for quick responses to crises, the long-term viability is contested. *Persevering* focuses on maintaining a status quo in business activities and does not focus on renewal. This contributes to a company's survival in the medium run if a crisis does not last too long. The strategic response of *innovating* allows strategic renewal in response to a crisis as it opens new opportunities for decision-making. It is therefore more suitable to sustaining a firm's long-term survival. Finally, *exit* refers to the discontinuation of a firm's business activity due to crisis. Literature with a focus on the connection between people and crisis management is rare. While Wenzel et al. (2021) review strategic management studies, a focus on the role people play in applying these strategic responses has been widely neglected (except for Dowell et al. 2011; Gartenberg/Pierce 2017). Other studies mainly connect to human resource development (HRD) (e.g. Reilly 2008; Wang 2008; Wang et al. 2009; Sheehan 2014; Vardarlıer 2016; Nizamidou/Vouzas 2018). Although strategically aligned learning, change, and performance interventions have the potential to support crisis management processes, Hutchins and Wang (2008) confirm in their literature review that the impacts of a crisis have not been sufficiently recognised in HRD research.

This raises questions about what managers in companies can do in terms of HR practices to respond effectively to a crisis. Israeli and Reichel (2003), for example, identified the following HR practices for crisis management in the Israeli hospitality industry: laying off employees and using unpaid vacation to reduce the labour force, decreasing the number of working hours per week, freezing pay rates, replacing high-tenure employees with new employees, and increased reliance on outsourcing. Based on this work, Lai and Wong (2020), in their recent study on the hotel industry in Macau during the Covid-19 pandemic, added another HR practice during a crisis, namely providing voluntary early retirement or resignation plans. Following a more strategic approach, Vardarlıer (2016) suggests considering HR practices as part of a crisis plan to reorganise and re-evaluate recruitment processes, job analysis, incentive schemes, and the focus on talent as well as the revision of short and long-term goals. However, questions as to whether these practices are suitable to specific business sectors such as banking or whether combining different HR practices into bundles are effective for crisis management remain unanswered. Only Teague and Roche (2014) addressed the importance of combining HR practices to cope with the Irish recession and identified three bodies of literature to show how firms use HR bundles in recessionary conditions. The authors suggest a combination of HR practices for employment stabilisation, responsible restructuring and pure downsizing as categories which incorporate specific recessionary bundles and adjustment programmes for crises (Teague/Roche 2014).

To summarize, studies show the need for HR practice bundles. However, since most scholars focus on recessionary HR practices, we believe that research so far comes too short of suggesting solutions for crises. Scholars have not sufficiently emphasised the role of people in implementing HR practices, nor have they examined the specific context of a transition economy.

Context of Bosnia: Covid-19 and the implications for businesses

The Bosnian government is divided in two entities – the Federation of Bosnia and Herzegovina (FBiH) and the Republika Srpska (RS). Like its counterparts around Europe, the Bosnian government restricted social life in mid-March 2020 to stop the pandemic and declared a state of emergency in both entities.

The focus of our study is on the FBiH, which is the larger entity with a more concentrated banking sector. The FBiH government urged employers to react and implement safety measures at work, reorganise working hours, use up annual leave and enable work from home to stem the repercussions from the lockdown (Chamber of Economy of FBiH 2020 a). However, the government itself only implemented limited measures to support businesses. Apart from a decree on intervention measures to support vulnerable sectors, little help has reached companies to date (Chamber of Economy of FBiH 2020 b). Therefore, the employers' association of FBiH and the chamber of economy of FBiH jointly developed a support initiative for companies, including co-financing of ongoing costs for businesses, a moratorium on loans, providing new loan arrangements under more favourable conditions and a deferral of tax payments (Chamber of Economy of FBiH 2020 c). In April 2020, the employers' association of FBiH initiated a survey of 761 companies to understand the severity of the pandemic related to businesses. Around one third of the surveyed companies had reduced their number of employees, and around half of the companies aimed to furlough at least 20 percent of staff by the end of 2020 (FBiH Employers' Association 2020). Furthermore, preliminary results from a survey of 100 companies by the University of Sarajevo during September and October 2020 show that over 80 percent of businesses report a decline in income and that almost 40 percent could not access governmental support. Over 80 percent had already laid off staff, while almost half of the companies surveyed introduced wage cuts that, in some cases, have been as high as 30 percent (Čizmić et al. 2020).

These results (in line with the previous studies outlined above) show that businesses apply common recessionary measures and that HR practices in crisis management focus on restructuring at the expense of the employees. By identifying different response strategies, we emphasise the role of people in implementing HR practices and show patterns of company survival. We suggest actionable, value-added principles in terms of HR practice bundles which can help companies achieve a horizontal fit.

Methodology

We chose group expert interviews with seven HR representatives in banks that operate in FBiH. The first and third author, and at least one company representative, were present in the interviews. We purposefully sampled the companies to include the largest players in the market. Based on previous experiences in other research projects involving financial companies in Bosnia, we relied on personal contacts as gatekeepers to access the HR departments. The banking sector in Bosnia is highly concentrated with only a few main actors, all of which are well represented in our sample. We collected our data in six banks in a two-month period from October to December 2020. Table 1 shows an overview of the company sample.

Table 1: Company sample

	A-Bank	B-Bank	C-Bank	D-Bank	E-Bank	F-Bank
Size	Large	Large	Large	Large	Large	Medium
Employees	450	360	500	354	434	150
Employees/HR	4	4	8	7	5	2

Source: Documents from company websites and interviews with HR representatives. Small: 0–50 employees, medium 50–250 employees, large over 250 employees

Based on a guide, we conducted semi-structured interviews that aimed to capture the changes in HR resulting from Covid-19. The guide was slightly adapted to the different banks. Our questions addressed general HR practices, changes due to the pandemic and crisis management in the banks. We asked questions openly but prompted the interviewees when necessary to learn about particular HR practices (e.g. pay and performance management or HR development). Interviews were conducted in Bosnian and lasted between 45 and 60 minutes. Table 2 gives an overview of the number of interviews and the position of the interview partners.

Table 2: Overview of group interviews conducted

Bank	Interview partners	Interviewers
A-Bank	– HR Director	
B-Bank	– HR Director – HR Business Partner	
C-Bank	– HR Director	– First and third author
D-Bank	– HR Business Partner	
E-Bank	– HR Director	
F-Bank	– HR Director	

Interviewees were between 36 and 60 years old, and all had a tertiary education. All interviews were audio-recorded and supplemented with detailed notes about the interview situation. Additional company data, such as annual reports from company websites, were provided by the interviewees.

Our research questions and interview topics followed a thematic analysis (Braun/Clarke 2006), using the software MAXQDA. Table 3 shows exemplary codes.

Table 3: Data representation (examples)

Themes	Second order constructs	First order constructs	Representative quotes
Impact of Covid-19 on HR in general	Workload	New tasks	"Even though some tasks were cancelled, the pandemic has brought new things (...). You now have some reporting to do that was not there before (...)." (HR Director, E-Bank)
	Digitalisation	Digital tools	"(...) even before the pandemic, the bank was in transition and our strategy is to go more towards digitalisation and towards any agile transformations. That was in general our strategy, even before the pandemic. The pandemic has only accelerated some things." (HR Director, E-Bank)
	Support	Employee needs	"Our long-term plan is to hire a psychologist. We all have a fear of infection, and we probably have some psychological consequences. (...)." (HR Business Partner, D-Bank)

Themes	Second order constructs	First order constructs	Representative quotes
Impact of Covid-19 on HR practices	HR recruitment	Video / online recruitment	"The newest practice is hiring via video. In some cases (...) in remote locations, we did the first round of interviews even via Viber." (HR Director, A-Bank)
	HR development	Changes in educational activities	"This year, we did not implement many of our plans due to the pandemic, from team building to classroom education." (HR Business Partner, D-Bank)

We started with an inductive analysis guided by our research question and interview guide to identify emerging patterns in our data. In this first coding step, we identified codes related to HR changes in general (such as digital tools) and changes in HR practices (such as video/online recruitment). In a second step, we merged the codes into second-order constructs relating to developments in HR (such as digitalisation) and the practices themselves (such as HR recruitment). Then, we developed themes by analysing similarities and differences in the companies (such as impact of Covid-19 on HR practices). Since we looked at the themes through the lens of strategic human resource management and crisis management, the last part of the coding process was deductive. In this phase, we noticed that the banks (contrary to the overall assumption of HR in Bosnia) had focused strongly on their company culture and on responsibility toward their employees. Overall, during this part of the coding process, it became clear that the crisis had not radically changed HR practices, but rather had amplified ongoing developments (such as those related to digitalisation). Furthermore, banks utilised innovative HR strategies to deal with the repercussions of the crisis.

Findings

The role of HR – creating a strong company culture and strategy implementation

Contrary to previous research on Bosnia (Vuk 2012; Rahimić/Vuk 2012), all HR departments had a strategic orientation, aligning an HR strategy with their business strategy. Overall, we saw two major areas where HR played a crucial role in the banks: 1) creating a strong company culture and 2) a strategic focus of HR.

When asked about the organisational climate, HR representatives emphasised a *strong company culture* as being crucial to cope with the repercussions of the crisis and to connect people to the organisation (see also Spicer, 2020):

"(...) You cannot feel the energy of people without physical contact. (...) We had to give up our annual party, team building, and leadership forum with a heavy heart. All of the fun stuff was not

available. (...) Since we could not socialise, a few colleagues from the bank gathered and went hiking for humanitarian purposes so as not to lose that spirit of ours where we still hang out and take care of each other." (HR Director, B-Bank)

Banks provided financial aid for Bosnian foundations during the pandemic, offered support packages for the most vulnerable groups in Bosnian society (e.g. pensioners) and most recently donated holiday gifts to children affected by the pandemic. The involvement of staff in designing such measures was decisive. Although voluntary, almost 70 percent of the employees in one bank (D-Bank) decided to donate a certain percentage of their salary to support NGOs early in the pandemic. According to HR representatives, these activities contributed to strengthening company culture and creating a better awareness of the banks as good corporate citizens in Bosnian society. This was crucial because the banks, according to the HR representatives, were under a lot of pressure from regulators early in the pandemic to ensure that customers faced as little repercussion from the crisis as possible.

The *strategic focus* in the banks was on HR practices that ensured a cultural fit, including a fit between company culture, recruitment, HR development and talent management. This reveals a transformation of the HR function in the past decade (starting in the early 2010s), which in Bosnia had previously been mostly operational. The change provided HR with more decision-making power and enabled banks to have stable responses during Covid-19. Our findings show that a strategic awareness, in combination with a strong company culture, allowed the banks to stay 'on course' throughout 2020. This resulted in limited changes to the overall strategy but drastic changes (at times) to the implementation of HR practices. Table 4 shows an overview of the HR practices before the pandemic and changes made during it.

Table 4: Overview of HR practices before pandemic and changes made during it

HR Practice	Before the pandemic/ Focus on	Changes during the pandemic/ Focus on
Recruitment, selection and succession planning	– Recruiting to achieve cultural fit – Talent as a challenge in general, due to emigration and the decreasing attractiveness of the banking sector	– Shift to online recruitment – Continuity in recruitment – Maintaining the number of employees – Recruiting of more specialised employees with digitalisation skills
Performance management and rewards	– Variable part of wages as key component – Precise key performance indicators, assessed either quarterly or yearly	– Postponement or cancellation – Guaranteeing pre-pandemic wages but cutting bonuses
HR development	– Continuous education and trainings – Team building and mentoring	– Shift to online trainings or postponement – New trainings for mental health and well-being

Impact of Covid-19 on HR – the same, only different?
Crisis management

Due to banking regulations, all banks had a 'business continuity plan' for crisis situations. However, in the early days of the pandemic banks had to adapt their plans quickly in order to be able to respond to pandemic-related challenges:

> *"We are quite well prepared compared to some other industries. Nobody could have predicted Covid, but in terms of crisis situations, such as earthquakes, flooding or economic crises, we have predictions and stress scenarios ready." (HR-Director, A-Bank)*

A crisis team that operated at the management level, with the HR directors as permanent members, underscores the nowadays strategic role of HR in the banks. Still, there were noteworthy differences in how crisis management was enforced. International banking groups had to follow very specific requirements from the headquarters such as sending the majority of staff home when the pandemic started and then gradually calling a specific percentage back at a later date. However, some headquarters only provided guidance and local banks were free to decide what worked best for their specific Bosnian context. Current information on the specific developments of the pandemic in Bosnia strengthened the strategic role of HR in Bosnian banks and resulted in joint crisis team management decisions with the headquarters.

Recruitment and succession planning

For several years, banks have struggled to find the right talent. *Recruiting* challenges were intensified during the pandemic, as the quote below shows:

> *"The biggest challenge is finding the right people. Covid has amplified this – the importance of people in some critical functions." (HR Director, A-Bank)*

Our interviewees saw several reasons for this situation, including decreasing attractiveness of the banking sector in the country, wide-spread emigration resulting in the loss of talent and a lack of people with new functional skills in IT and data management, both of which are now needed in the banking sector. A recent Gallup survey (2020) showed that Bosnia has suffered severely from brain drain with 40 percent of highly educated residents leaving the country. Hence, banks have implemented HR practices to position themselves as attractive employers. These have included offering relatively high wages, increasing employee engagement and providing job security in Bosnia's volatile labour market, all of which are targeted at keeping employees and attracting new ones.

The impact of the pandemic on the recruitment process itself, however, has been limited. Although recruitment was put on hold in the first weeks of the pandemic, it was quickly resumed in May 2020. Now, it is conducted completely online via different platforms. The banks have not (yet) changed their *succession* plans and continue to recruit employees in the same intensity as before the pandemic. In some cases, the focus shifted to more specific functions. For example, candidates with knowledge in digitalisation are now more sought after (see below). Interestingly, because most had been in reorganisation for several years prior to the pandemic, banks did not have to furlough or lay-off employees:

> *"We have not changed the number of employees. But we are in a continuous process of adaptation with the aim to have as little employees as possible to deliver the tasks. In 2019, we had a reorganisation where we have cut the number of people." (HR Director, B-Bank)*

Performance management and rewards

Performance management was an important HR practice in the banks. Since the outbreak of the pandemic, however, most banks have adapted how they measure the performance of employees. While some HR professionals indicated a desire to continue online performance management, this was completely suspended for 2020 in other banks.

Predominant changes in *rewards* refer to a reduction or cut of the variable component. All banks reported that bonuses would not be paid out. The management board of the A-Bank decided to reduce their wages until the end of 2020:

> *"We have cut wages only in management. They [the management] have decided this [to cut their wages only]. This was a nice gesture, you know. When you have limited income, you cut the luxury [not the employee wages]." (HR Director, A-Bank)*

Additionally, some of the banks limited benefits such as reimbursing food or travel. Wages for employees were not changed in any of the banks, although all HR representatives doubted that this would remain the case after 2020. Finally, costs were also saved due to limited travel as well as trainings that were moved online.

HR development

In general, most of the banks have an elaborate *HR development* which includes months-long induction programmes, trainings and other educational activities. HR representatives confirmed the need for continuous learning and development as being key for survival in the market (see also Gold/Smith 2003).

With the pandemic, HR development was moved online or stopped completely with no classroom education throughout 2020. Team building events were also cancelled. However, interviewees mentioned some new activities. HR departments started to offer trainings for the mental health and well-being of employees and shifted their overall focus towards more communication with employees (as we show further below). Besides the changes to the regular HR practices, the HR departments introduced new HR practices and combined existing ones in innovative ways to achieve a horizontal fit.

Creating HR systems with innovative HR practice bundles
Embracing digitalisation as a new prerequisite

As of March 2020, all banks had shifted their operations towards working from home. This was achieved quickly (e.g. in some cases everyone had a laptop and access to the banks' networks within 48 hours). Yet while the banks welcomed the opportunity for digitalisation, the context they operated in made implementation difficult. The domestic bank struggled most with working from home, as sourcing laptops for employees was based on time-consuming public tenders. The procurement process was still ongoing during the time of the interview, which shows that the domestic bank is much more dependent on the norms and regulations of the specific Bosnian context. Although all interviewees acknowledged that still a lot is to be done on paper, our findings show an openness towards digitalisation which impacts HR practices. There was consensus that banks are ready to have most HR processes digitalised, but the context often does not allow for it. As the HR director of B-Bank stated: "This is how our country is!"

According to the HR representatives, some changes regarding digitalisation will be permanent, including working from home, more online meetings and online recruitment. As of 2021, all banks will permanently allow employees to work from home for one or two pre-defined days per week. Experience from 2020 showed that an overwhelming number of employees valued the flexibility of working from home if they had the right equipment. All HR representatives acknowledged the missing legal framework for working from home and wished for better regulation from the government.

Digitalisation has also had a direct impact on talent management as some of the banks have started to search for talent in the field of data management and digital transformation. On-boarding and including such specialists into the company culture were seen as crucial steps to be taken in person. Thus, HR representatives hope to model respective HR practices on pre-pandemic approaches to strengthen the company culture.

Combining communication and support measures to enhance employee engagement

HR professionals overwhelmingly noted that employee engagement was not affected negatively by the pandemic. Because of digitalisation, employees actually became more flexible in terms of working hours and availability. According to the HR professionals, there was no indication of a higher turnover or absenteeism due to the pandemic. At the same time, they focused more on communication to maintain employee engagement (e.g. regular phone calls or catch ups with HR representatives or line managers) (see also Nyberg et al. 2021).

In addition, several banks provided employee counselling with psychologists. The pandemic showed that a lack of personal communication and structure resulted in fear or unease about the repercussions of the virus. Mental health support for employees is not common in Bosnian companies, but banks took on an innovative role in recognising the need for such support. Resources formerly used for trainings and meetings onsite were shifted towards more 'care work':

> *"Our long-term plan is to hire a psychologist. We all have a fear of infection, and we probably have some psychological consequences. Some long-term plan is to have a psychologist, so that employees can get in touch, and we enable this for them." (HR Business Partner, D-Bank)*

In addition to entry and exit interviews, one bank developed more direct communication with employees:

> *"We decided to do a 'stay interview' because some other things failed or were moved because of Covid. (...) The goal is to get feedback primarily about satisfaction in the bank, the job, whether they like it or not, whether they feel engaged, etc. In order to this, HR must build its credibility with both top management and employees so that they have confidence (to share information). (HR Director, C-Bank)*

Overall, the HR departments strengthened their role as a service provider by staying in the office and being available for employees' concerns:

"We have an open-door policy, we implemented this as we have seen that people have become more closed up (at home). Communication during Covid is our main challenge". (HR Business Partner, D-Bank)

Coping with the long-term impact of the pandemic

While it is difficult to anticipate the long-term impact of the pandemic, current projections for Bosnia show an economic downfall lasting until at least 2022 (CBBIH, 2020) and unemployment is expected to rise. In the banks interviewed, this had not yet been the case. No recessionary HR practices (e.g. pay cuts) had yet been implemented, although this could change in the future.

In terms of strategic orientation, none of the banks had developed a pandemic-specific HR strategy. An overwhelming number of interviewees perceived the pandemic as a 'one-off' event and expected a normalisation for the Bosnian economy within the next year or two. But the interviewees also emphasised the need for HR to alleviate the impact of the virus. Apart from creating an HR system with complementary HR practices, HR representatives have to defend their crucial role in the companies by ensuring that their planning will not suffer in the months ahead. A more severe impact in the following years is expected across the banks:

"It is possible that there will be cuts in the banking sector. The pandemic has had a different impact on different banks, not everyone is affected in the same way. But we will all have to 'tighten our belts', as they say." (HR Director, C-Bank)

Discussion

In this study, we analyse how banks respond to the Covid-19 pandemic through their HR practices. Our findings provide insight into HR practices in the banking sector before and during the pandemic and show that a horizontal fit in HR systems can help companies survive a crisis. Below, we outline concrete measures in terms of actionable principles for the development of an HR system in a transition economy. These can add value to companies and do not have to be implemented at the expense of employees.

Implications for theory and practice

First and foremost, our study contributes to the literature on HRM as well as crisis management. In contrast to earlier studies, we show that HR in Bosnia has a more strategic role and focuses intensely on fostering company culture. HRM developed over the last decade and became a crucial function in the banks' strategies (see also Bešić/Hirt, 2020). Admittedly, because banks had already strategically implemented crisis management due to regulations and previous crises, we cannot confirm that the Covid-19 pandemic was the trigger for a more strategic orientation. Ascendant research, however, shows that HR is central to organisational responses to the pandemic and that it can contribute to operational and strategic success (Collings et al. 2021 a, b). Seen within this context, a focus on strengthening the strategic role of HR seems to serve the banks well. Overall, the study shows that banks were better prepared than other sectors.

Second, we demonstrate that strengthening company culture via HR practice bundles can support a company in crisis management. This addresses calls for more research on, specifically, the impact of the Covid-19 pandemic on company culture (Spicer 2020) and on the role of management research, more generally, in addressing the repercussions of the pandemic (Muzio/Doh 2021). A focus on a bundle of HR practices that is innovative and fosters employee engagement – for example, digital recruiting, communication, and support measures – can strengthen resilience. To engage employees effectively, communication needs to be authentic and continuous (Nyberg et al. 2021). Our findings confirm HR practices for employment stabilisation, as described by Teague and Roche (2014), with no compulsory lay-offs but ongoing training for new positions and extensive communication. Interestingly, contrary to downsizing and pure restructuring (Teague/Roche 2014) we did not discern recessionary HR practices in the Bosnian banking sector, but we show the need to combine HR practices into HR systems, as one single HR practice is not considered viable to cope with the pandemic. Contrary to earlier studies that have focused on retrenchment programmes in the hospitality industry (Israeli/Reichel 2003; Lai/Wong 2020), our findings also show that high-commitment HR systems are suitable for the Bosnian banking sector to respond to the acute pressures caused by the pandemic. Linking to Vardarlıer (2016), the pandemic led to a reorganisation of online recruitment processes, incentive schemes without bonuses and an even stronger focus on talent.

Third, we illustrate that all banks have responded to the pandemic by mainly following a *persevering* strategy (Wenzel et al. 2021), that is, keeping the status quo based on high-commitment HR practices. Although some banks stopped providing specific benefits (e.g. reimbursing travel expenses), overall salaries of employees stayed the same. Additionally, the A-Bank's management took a voluntary pay cut, but did not force this onto the employees. The fact that banks did not use HR practices to lay-off jobs or reduce wages in difficult times gave security to employees, which has increased loyalty to the employer and commitment to work. The small number of work absences, which were not higher compared to pre-pandemic numbers, and the willingness to work from home – despite isolation or with mild symptoms related to the virus – shows that this strategy works. Notwithstanding this positive development, we expect more profound changes in compensation in the long run, depending on how the crisis unfolds.

Parallel to the *persevering* response, we identify some indication of long-term strategic renewal and hence an *innovating* strategy (Wenzel et al. 2021) as companies include new HR practices. Here, concern for people and for their safety play a major role. For the banks, a strong crisis management which helps to react quickly and strengthen employee communication – between HR departments, line managers and their teams – are key to successfully adapt to the circumstances of the pandemic. HR acts as a change agent, and our findings show that bundling employee communication, online psychological training and digital recruiting have been successful so far. Due to the solutions digitalisation can offer, many banks were able to continue work, at least partially (Mora Cortez/Johnston 2020). As a result, the current pandemic accelerated digitalisation processes that were already happening in the banking sector.

Finally, the banks do not see the need to adopt a new HR strategy (yet). Persevering with the status quo and the innovation of some HR practices in response to the pandemic, are perceived as being compatible with the existing strategic orientation of the organisation. These include predominantly working from home with more digitalisation, but also strengthening the company culture by improving succession planning – specifically for crucial positions in risk management and digital transformation – and non-recessionary HR practices in crisis management (e.g continuous training). The interviews clearly show that because the banking sector has been in constant flux since the last economic crisis, banks have learned to react quickly to a downfall in revenues. Hence, quick reactions to the pandemic, in combination with innovative HR bundles, let banks emerge stronger from the crisis (at least in the short term).

Since we show that a strategic combination of HR bundles can be helpful for crisis management, our study has implications for HRM in the banking industry located in transition economies. Crises do not always require recessionary HR practices. Based on our findings, we propose HR systems that focus on stabilisation and the strengthening of company culture, enhancing employee engagement, and promoting communication and innovation in HR development, all of which can lead to resilience.

We further recommend using more digitalised HR practices in recruitment and offering more benefits such as working from home. These are cost-effective and easy to implement. The gains, moreover, are immediate. In this way, our proposed principles are actionable and can add value to a company in terms of employee engagement. However, since they are easily transferable to other companies and can develop into best practices, only the development of an HR system with a horizontal fit of HR practices will help banks to best manoeuvre through a crisis.

Limitations and future research directions

Although we address the main challenges of banks and their HR practices during the pandemic, we acknowledge that this study has several limitations. First, due to the current nature of the topic, the study was conducted in a short amount of time and with a small number of interviews. However, we included the main players in the banking sector and our interviewees are HR representatives with the most expertise on the subject. Second, we conducted all interviews in Bosnian and despite a meticulous translation of quotes we cannot fully eliminate a translation bias. To remedy this, the first and third author analysed all interviews, translated quotes into English and re-translated them into Bosnian to ensure a coherent meaning across languages. Third, since we only interviewed managers, we missed out on the employees' views on the implemented HR practice changes. We show a positive perspective of employee engagement without knowing if HR professionals gloss things over. We are also aware that employee commitment can stem from several other reasons not rooted in HR practices, including the fear of losing employment, which can create anxiousness and make employees overcompensate (e.g. Arora/Suri 2020). Finally, we are aware that a contextual analysis sets general limits to broader generalisation. Still, with our focus on the transition economy context and its banking sector, we highlight the relevance of context-specific studies, which can provide much needed actionable principles to companies left out of governmental support.

For future research, we recommend incorporating the employees' views to get a more balanced picture on perseverance and innovating responses for HR crisis management. We see the need for research in the context of transition economies to better understand how other countries and sectors cope with the repercussions of the pandemic. We have already started to work on a comparative survey in transition and developed economies in Central and Eastern Europe to provide a more holistic picture on the impact of Covid-19 on HR work and the challenges and responses in different sectors (Poór et al. 2021). Finally, since crises reoccur and companies consequently must work on the readjustment of their HR practice fit, we encourage research on HR practices in combination with resource and coordination flexibility (see also Wright/Snell 1998). Following up on our findings, companies – not only in transition economies – could benefit from theoretical guidance on how to better cope with crisis in a dynamic business environment. Our findings thus contribute to counteract the often-criticised value-added gap (Kaufman 2012), or the idea that researched topics are neither relevant nor provide an added value for the world of practice.

Conclusions

This study addressed the question of how banks in Bosnia respond to the Covid-19 pandemic through their HR practices. Bosnian banks have developed a more sophisticated and strategic HR approach and have shifted the development of HR from a merely operative function to a strategic asset. Pre-existing strategies for crisis management provide a solid basis to meet challenges of the pandemic. Bosnian banks have reacted to the changes in the business environment by innovating and adapting their HR practices. Although the pandemic portrays a situation of crisis, Bosnian banks have not implemented recessionary HR practices but have counted on stabilisation which can be achieved by digitally supported HR practices. Reaching a horizontal fit as a sustainable pattern for survival has not been fully implemented. While digital support of HR practices and introducing benefits for employees such as working from home are actionable and easy to implement, a better linkage of recruiting, performance management and HR development practices into sophisticated HR systems is still necessary. Both crisis management and strategic human resource management can provide necessary theoretical guidance for companies on how to successfully manage the changes brought on by the pandemic (see also Collings et al. 2021 a, b).

References

Arora, P./Suri, D. (2020): Redefining, relooking, redesigning, and reincorporating HRD in the post Covid 19 context and thereafter, in: Human Resource Development International, 23, 4, 438–451.

Arthur, J. B. (1994): Effects of human resource systems on manufacturing performance and turn-over, in: Academy of Management Journal, 37, 670–667.

Barney, J. B./Wright, P. M. (1998): On becoming a strategic partner: The role of human resources in gaining competitive advantage, in: Human Resource Management, 37, 1, 31–46.

Bešić, A./Hirt, C. (2020) Human resource practices diffusion of multinational companies in the Western Balkans: institutional distance and role of subsidiaries. Paper presented at EURAM 2020, 4–6 December 2020 (online).

Bešić, A./Ortlieb, R. (2019): Expatriates of host-country origin in South-Eastern Europe: Management rationales in the finance sector, in European Management Review, 16, 667-681.

Bešić, A./Hirt, C. (2016): Diversity management across borders: The role of the national context, in: Equality, Diversity and Inclusion: An International Journal, 35, 2, 123–135.

Boxall, P./Purcell, J. (2016): Strategy and Human Resource Management. Palgrave, London.

Braun, V./Clarke, V. (2006): Using thematic analysis in psychology, in: Qualitative Research in Psychology, 3, 2, 77–101.

Carnevale, J. B./Hatak, I. (2020): Employee adjustment and well-being in the era of Covid-19: Implications for human resource management, in: Journal of Business Research, 116, 183–187.

CBBIH (2020): Projection of a stronger recovery only at the end of 2022 (*Projekcija snažnijeg oporavka tek krajem 2022. Godine*), available at: https://www.cbbh.ba/press/ShowNews/1302 (accessed on 21 December 2020)

Chamber of Economy of FBiH (2020 a): Information for businesses – corona virus (Covid 19) (*Informacije za privrednike – koronavirus (Covid 19)*), available at: http://www.kfbih.com/vijesti-vezane-za-korona-virus (accessed on 27 October 2020)

Chamber of Economy of FBiH (2020 b): Decree on intervention measures to support vulnerable sectors of the FBiH economy during the Covid-19 pandemic (*Uredba o interventnim mjerama za podršku ugroženim sektorima privrede FBiH u okolnostima pandemije Covid-19*), available at: http://www.kfbih.com/uredba-o-interventnim-mjerama-za-podrsku-ugrozenim-sektorima-privrede-fbih-u-okolnostima-pandemije-c (accessed on 28 October 2020)

Chamber of Economy of FBiH (2020 c): Representatives of the Chamber of Economy of and the FBiH Employers' Association hold an extraordinary meeting (*Održan vanredni sastanak predstavnika Privredne/Gospodarske komore FBiH i Udruženja poslodavaca FBiH*), available at: http://www.kfbih.com/odrzan-vanredni-sastanak-predstavnika-privredne-gospodarske-komore-fbih-i-udruzenja-poslodavaca-fbih (accessed on 27 October 2020)

Čizmić, E./Softić, S./Šestić, M./Hrnjić, A. (2020): The impact of the Covid-19 pandemic on doing business in BiH (*Uticaj Covid-19 pandemije na poslovanje u BiH*). Working Paper, University of Sarajevo.

Cohen, D. J. (2007): The very separate worlds of academic and practitioner publications in human resource management: reasons for the divide and concrete solutions for bridging the gap, in: Academy of Management Journal, 50, 5, 1013–1019.

Collings, D. G./McMackin, J./Nyberg, A. J./Wright, P. M. (2021 a): Strategic human resource management and COVID-19: Emerging challenges and research opportunities, in: Journal of Management Studies, 58, 1378–1382.

Collings, D. G./Nyberg, A. J./Wright, P. M./McMackin, J. (2021 b): Leading through paradox in a COVID-19 world: Human resources comes of age, in: Human Resource Management Journal, 31, 819–833.

DeNisi, A. S./Wilson, M. S./Biteman J. (2014): Research and practice in HRM: a historical perspective, in: Human Resource Management Review, 24, 3, 219–231.

Diebold, F. X. (2020): Real-time economic activity: Exiting the great recession and entering the pandemic recession, in: NBER Working Paper Series, Working Paper 2742.

FBiH Employers' Association (2020): Assessment of the economic impact of Covid-19 in the Federation of BiH (*Procjena ekonomskog učinka Covid-19 u Federaciji BiH*). FBiH Employers' Association, Sarajevo.

Gallup (2020): Potential Net Migration Index, available at: https://news.gallup.com/migration/interactive.aspx (accessed on 29 March 2021).

Gartenberg, C./Pierce, L. (2017): Subprime governance: Agency costs in vertically integrated banks and the 2008 mortgage crisis, in: Strategic Management Journal, 38, 300–321.

Gold, J./Smith, V. (2003): Advances towards a learning movement. Translations at work, in: Human Resource Development International, 6, 2, 139–154.

Hutchins, H. M./Wang, J. (2008): Organisational crisis management and human resource development: A review of the literature and implications to HRD research and practice, in: Advances in Developing Human Resources, 10, 3, 310–330.

Israeli, A. A./Reichel, A. (2003): Hospitality crisis management practices: the Israeli case, in: International Journal of Hospitality Management, 22, 4, 353–372.

Johns Hopkins University (2021): Coronavirus Resource Center, available at: https://coronavirus.jhu.edu/ (accessed on 02 July 2021).

Kaufman, B. E. (2012): Strategic human resource management research in the United States: A failing grade after 30 years? in: Academy of Management Perspectives, 26, 2, 12–36.

Lado, A. A./Wilson, M.C. (1994): Human resource systems and sustained competitive advantage: A competency-based perspective, in: Academy of Management Review, 19, 4, 699–727.

Lai, I.K.W./Wong, J.W.C. (2020): Comparing crisis management practices in the hotel industry between initial and pandemic stages of Covid-19, in: International Journal of Contemporary Hospitality Management, 32, 10, 3135–3156.

Lebrenz, C. (2020): Strategy and HRM. Concepts and instruments for implementation in companies. (*Strategie und Personalmanagement. Konzepte und Instrumente zur Umsetzung im Unternehmen*). 2. Edition. Wiesbaden: Springer.

Mora Cortez, R./Johnston, W. J. (2020): The Coronavirus crisis in B2B settings: Crisis uniqueness and managerial implications based on social exchange theory, in: Industrial Marketing Management, 88, 125–135.

Muzio, D./Doh, J. (2021): COVID-19 and the future of management studies. Insights from leading scholars, in: Journal of Management Studies, 58, 1371–1377.

Nizamidou, C. / Vouzas, F. (2018): MHR. Providing a new perspective in HR in terms of crisis management, in: Int. Journal of Business Science and Applied Management, 13, 1, 15–25.

Nyberg, A. J./Shaw, J. D./Zhu, J. (2021): The people still make the (remote work-) place: Lessons from a pandemic, in: Journal of Management, 47, 8, 1967–1976.

Ortlieb, R./Rahimić, Z./Hirt, C./Bešić, A./Bieber, F. (2019): Diversity and equality in Bosnia and Herzegovina. Limits to legislation, public debate and workplace practices, in: Equality, Diversity and Inclusion: An International Journal, 38, 7, 763–778.

Ostrom, E. (1990): Governing the Commons. The Evolution of Institutions for Collective Action. Cambridge: Cambridge University Press.

Pfeffer, J. (1994): Competitive advantage through people. Boston: Harvard Business School Press.

Poór, J./Zaharie, M./Kerekes,K/Szeiner, Z./Ladislav, M./Szabó, K/Bešić, A./Rahimić, Z./Hirt C./Ilieva S. (2021): Human Resource Management during the Covid-19 pandemic: An empirical research in six CEE countries. Presentation at the International Scientific Conference of the Faculty of Business Management of the University of Economics in Bratislava and The CRANET Research Network on International Human Resource Management "Economics, Finance and Business Management – 2021".

Rahimić, Z./Vuk, S. (2012): Evaluation the effects of employee education in BH. companies. Proceedings of 6th International Conference of the School of Economics and Business „Beyond the Economic Crisis: Lessons Learned and Challenges Ahead", 1044–1057, Sarajevo.

Reilly, AH. (2008): The role of human resource development competencies in facilitating effective crisis communication, in: Advances in Developing Human Resources, 10, 3, 331–351.

Ritter, T./Pedersen, C. L. (2020): Analyzing the impact of the coronavirus crisis on business models, in: Industrial Marketing Management, 88, 214–224.

Schuler, R. S. (1992): Linking the people with the strategic needs of the business, in: Organisational Dynamics, 21, 1, 18–32.

Schuler, R. S./Jackson, S. E. (1987): Linking competitive strategies with human resource management practices, in: The Academy of Management Executive, 1, 3, 207–219.

Sheehan, M. (2014): Investment in training and development in times of uncertainty, in: Advances in Developing Human Resources, 16, 1, 13–33.

Spicer, A. (2020): Organisational culture and COVID-19, in: Journal of Management Studies, 57, 1737–1740.

Teague, P./Roche, W.K. (2014): Recessionary bundles: HR practices in the Irish economic crisis, in: Human Resource Management Journal, 24, 176–192.

Trougakos, J. P./Chawla, N./McCarthy, J. M. (2020): Working in a pandemic: Exploring the impact of COVID-19 health anxiety on work, family, and health outcomes, in: Journal of Applied Psychology, 105, 11, 1234–1245.

Vardarlıer, P. (2016): Strategic approach to human resource management during crisis, in: Procedia – Social and Behavioral Sciences, 235, 463–472.

Vuk, S. (2012): Continuous education of employees for strengthening the competitiveness of companies *(Kontinuirano obrazovanje zaposlenih u funkciji jačanja konkurentnosti preduzeća)*, IC Mostar: Univerzitet Džemal Bijedić.

Wang J. (2008): Developing organisational learning capacity in crisis management, in: Advances in Developing Human Resources, 10, 3, 25–445.

Wang, J./Hutchins, H. M./ Garavan, T. N. (2009): Exploring the strategic role of human resource development in organisational crisis management, in: Human Resource Development Review, 8, 1, 22–53.

Wenzel, M./Stanske, S./Lieberman, M. B. (2021): Strategic responses to crisis, in: Strategic Management Journal, 42, O16-O27

Wright, P. M./Snell, S. A. (1998): Toward a unifying framework for exploring fit and flexibility in strategic human resource management. in: Academy of Management Review, 23, 4, 756–772.

Wright, P. M./Dunford, B. B./Snell, S.t A. (2001): Human resources and the resource based view of the firm, in: Journal of Management, 27, 701–721.

Wright, P. M./McMahan, G. C. (1992): Theoretical perspectives for strategic human resource management, in: Journal of Management, 18, 2, 295–320.

Wright, P. M./McMahan, G. C./Mc Williams, A. (1994): Human resources and sustained competitive advantage: A resource-based perspective, in: International Journal of Human Resource Management, 5, 2, 301–326.

The response of Hungarian SMEs to the Covid-19 pandemic: a Resilience Adaption Model[*]

Tim Gittins, Gergely Freész, Loretta Huszák[**]

Abstract

The Covid-19 pandemic has resulted in unprecedented uncertainty for small and medium sized enterprises (SMEs). The aim of this study is therefore to assess resilience based responses adopted by SMEs in Hungary as a globally integrated medium sized economy. With research on business related response of SMEs to the pandemic in the CEE (Central and Eastern Europe) region relatively scarce, a qualitative approach was applied to 22 SME managers in Hungary through a series of narrative-based interviews. Consequently, an adaption model was identified whereby six resilience modes were classified based on SME managerial response to continuing pandemic driven uncertainty

Keywords: Resilience Adaption, Covid-19, Hungary, SMEs
JEL Codes: H12, M00, O52.

1. Introduction

The Covid-19 pandemic embodies a 'transboundary' phenomenon (Boin, 2018) whereby its economic effects are transmitted through global supply chains and trading activities. Globalisation entails locally based SMEs acting as ancillary organisations and as customers for multinational enterprises (MNEs) with global scale. Thus the 'liability of smallness' (Freeman, Carroll and Hannan, 1983), in terms of SMEs generally possessing lower resource levels than larger counterparts is crucial in their response to the Covid-19 pandemic.

The pandemic is moreover not representative of a 'single event' crisis such as an earthquake. While SME crisis management has emerged as a research field in recent years (i.e. Cucculelli and Peruzzi, 2020; Doern, Williams and Vorley, 2019: Herbane, 2019) it assumes recovery to a pre-crisis situation. In spite of vaccination efforts inviting alleviation of the economic effects of the pandemic

---

[*] Received: 21.12.20, Accepted: 24.9.21,1 revision.
[**] *Tim Gittins,* PhD, Associate Professor, Institute for the Development of Enterprises, Corvinus University Budapest. Email: tim.gittins@uni-corvinus.hu. Main research Interests: Entrepreneurship in the CEE region, Informal and Ethnic Entrepreneurship, Human Capital, Social Capital, SME Crisis Management, Entrepreneurial Ecosystems, SME Internationalization, Organizational Learning in SMEs
Gergely Freész, PhD Student, Institute for the Development of Enterprises, Corvinus University Budapest. Email: gergely.freesz@uni-corvinus.hu. Main research Interests: Institutional Venture Capital and Entrepreneurial Relations, Internal Structures of SMEs Receiving Venture Capital Investment
Loretta Huszák, PhD, Assistant Professor, Institute for the Development of Enterprises, Corvinus University Budapest. Email: loretta.huszak@uni-corvinus.hu. Main research Interests: Innovation Management, IP Commercialization, Small Business Development, International Business

at time of writing (May 2021) it is unlikely to cease entirely in the foreseeable future (WHO 2021), thus underlining its overall transformative nature in terms of ongoing general uncertainty for SMEs considered as more vulnerable than larger counterparts.

The aim of this study is therefore framed in terms of organisational resilience (Conz and Magnani, 2020; Darkow, 2019; Duchek, 2020; Hillmann and Guenther, 2021) assuming ongoing adaption by SMEs to continuous pandemic related uncertainty with no immediate prospect of reversion to a pre-pandemic operational environment. The pandemic also forms a previously unexperienced event in living memory to provide motivation for this study to focus upon 'lived experience' based response of SMEs located in Hungary's transitional socio-economic context. Moreover, continually emerging business related research on the pandemic tends to focus on strategic responses of MNEs (multinational enterprises) and insufficiently on those of SMEs (Etemad, 2020).

Extant literature also reveals a paucity of work specifically related to business related effects of the pandemic in the CEE region which is characterised by domination of foreign-based MNEs, lower income levels than Western Europe and a lack of macro-economic convergence with the Eurozone (Artner, 2018; Beck, 2020). Hungary, acting as a national research unit for this study, is a relatively medium sized transitional economy with a strong domestically focused SME sector which is however strongly exposed to the international nature of the pandemic (Karácsony, 2020).

Against this background, a qualitatively oriented grounded research approach (Corbin and Strauss, 2014) was selected given its conduciveness to the relative newness of the pandemic whereby unique narrative drawn from SME key respondents is generated to inductively derive insights. Moreover, given the continuous nature of the pandemic it was decided that a deductively oriented quantitative survey would be only be of use when it has substantially abated and only then provide a relatively summative appraisal.

This paper proceeds by initially outlining the situational background of the pandemic in Hungary. This is followed by presentation of a conceptual framework as a basis for subsequent research questions. The data collection process applied to SMEs in different industrial sectors is then outlined followed by explanation of the grounded theory methodological approach. Coded findings are then presented and thematised to guide development of the resilience adaption model and to address research questions in the subsequent discussion section. A variety of response modes were identified which may act as a basis for further research and policy development focusing on SME resilience assuming relative permanence of the pandemic.

2. Situational Background – Covid-19 in Hungary

The Covid-19 pandemic emerged in Hungary in mid-March 2020 when a period of economic 'lockdown' was imposed. Hungary recorded a lower rate of infections and deaths in the early phase of the pandemic than most neighboring countries in the CEE region (WHO, 2020). The lockdown was eased in late May 2020 and a continuing substantial increase in new infections began in mid-August, peaking in December and only decelerating in early 2021 (WHO, 2021). Lockdown restrictions were re-imposed in November and extended in March 2021 as a dramatic 'third wave' of infections emerged and then subsided. While a vaccination programme commenced in February 2021, Hungary maintains relatively high new infection and mortality rates compared with Western European countries and immediate neighboring countries (WHO 2021).

Hungarian SMEs contributed over 54 per cent of value added to national GDP in 2018 and 68.9 per cent of national employment in 2017 with 24 per cent of total Hungarian exports accounted for by SMEs in 2016 (European Commission, 2019) underlining the relative economic importance of the sector. In 2016 The World Bank (2019) estimated exports of goods and services to be nearly 84.9 per cent of GDP and that of imports to be 80.5 per cent in 2018 to illustrate a strong extent of integration with the global economy.

The pandemic's initial economic effect is reflected in a decline of 34.6 per cent in the volume of goods exported over March-April 2020 and of Hungarian GDP by 13.3 per cent in the second quarter of 2020 which reduced to a decline of 3.5 per cent in the final quarter (Hungarian Central Statistical Office, 2021). Hungarian GDP declined by 5.3 per cent overall in 2020 whereas GDP for the entire European Union (EU) declined by 0.5 percent over the same period (Eurostat, 2021). While this data is arguably reflective of a more severe effect of the pandemic on CEE transitional economies, Hungarian GDP is predicted by the European Commission (2021) to increase by 4.0 percent in 2021 and by 5.0 per cent in 2022. In comparison GDP growth for the entire EU of 3.7 per cent in 2021 and 3.9 per cent in 2022 is predicted, thus presenting a slightly more optimistic macro-economic outlook for Hungary.

While the preceding data infers a dramatic effect on SMEs due to the liability of smallness (Freeman, Carroll and Hannan, 1983) official sources do not reveal bankruptcy data whereby business failure could be directly attributed to the pandemic. Governmental support is however available but measures are largely not specifically focused on SMEs and a direct grant scheme was implemented in May 2020 to cover SME working capital costs (European Commission, 2020). A general loan moratorium applicable to all enterprises and individuals was also introduced and SMEs are otherwise eligible for employment subsidy support available to all enterprises (European Commission, 2020).

In overall terms, data suggests that perhaps due to transitional status Hungary incurred a stronger macro-economic impact of the pandemic's emergence than the European Union as a whole. This aspect partially forms rationale for conceptual development for the research approach applied in this study.

3. Conceptual Framework

While crisis management research has developed in recent decades in response to single event crises it is arguably of limited use in addressing the continuous nature of the Covid-19 pandemic. Epidemiological knowledge of the virus is still developing with predictions of it leading to an endemic or albeit less lethal quasi-permanent state (WHO, 2021). Thus assuming immediate return to pre-pandemic operating conditions is improbable, an implicit need for adaption to new conditions by organisations arises thereby emphasising the role of resilience as a cognitive phenomenon encompassing adaption to changing conditions beyond that of mere survival.

Definitions of resilience vary but it is etymologically taken to derive from the Latin verb 'resiline' translated as 'recoiling' or 'rebounding' (Darkow, 2019). In an organisational context resilience may be viewed as the ability to cope with adverse operating conditions (Wildavsky, 2004). Conz and Magnani (2020) suggest organisational resilience assumes paths of absorption of initial experience and adaption to new conditions. Hillman and Guenther (2021) further develop this theme by suggesting organisational resilience leads to growth through renewal, adaption and learning from initial or 'lived' experience.

The current pandemic has precedents in the SARS epidemic in China and Hong Kong in 2002–03 and the MERS epidemic in South Korea in 2015 as providing evidence of resilience driven business response. While the medical and economic impacts of both cases were geographically limited, a reduction of demand in specific sectors such as tourism resulting from changed consumer behavior due to SARS was noted by Lee and McKibbin (2004). MERS is furthermore described by Kim, Yoon and Jung (2017) as a 'catastrophic' event, given there was no recognised medical treatment for the condition, thereby inviting parallels with the Covid-19 pandemic in terms of ongoing macro-economic uncertainty.

Limited reference to prior 'transboundary' medical emergencies nonetheless drives consideration of business related response to the current pandemic. This is particularly relevant for those SMEs with international exposure through supply chain linkages (Etemad, 2020). Specific pandemic related challenges for SMEs typically lie in drastic loss of domestic and export markets and global supply chain disruption (Ratten, 2020). Such challenges may moreover be assumed to be intermittent with continuing cycles of infection waves and lockdowns.

Relatedly, Wenzel Stanske and Lieberman (2020) formed a typology for general response forms of businesses to the emergence of Covid-19. This consisted of *retrenchment* entailing structured resource control, *perseverance* focusing on survival and *innovation* whereby new products and services are developed. Eggers (2020) suggested SMEs face a 'chicken and egg' challenge in Covid-19 conditions in that restricted resources may lead to improved performance through enhanced leanness but they are however less inclined to assume risk. Kraus *et al* (2020) conducted a qualitative survey of family owned SMEs in five central European countries in the early pandemic phase to develop a model of forms of strategic response ranging from short term *ad hoc* to longer term measures thus producing a formative framework for SME based resilience. Kuckertz *et al* (2020) also conducted a formative qualitative study of the response of German startup companies to Covid-19, to suggest that while firms leveraged resources effectively in the immediate term, leanness might reduce long term innovation potential to infer the presence of resilience related dilemmas faced by SMEs.

Economic transition in the CEE region in the early 1990s featured large scale privatisation and creation of substantial SME sectors. This presented cognitive challenges in the form of adaption to market based entrepreneurial norms not embodied in the previous centrally planned economic system (Welter and Smallbone, 2011). Early transition thus arguably acts as a precedent for SME resilience adaption in the current pandemic in that firms were largely confronted with volatile market conditions upon inception. Andor and Tóth (2018) examined performance related response to the global financial crisis (GFC) of 2008–10 in the CEE region and found that smaller firms were more exposed to market related volatility. Moreover, Stojcic (2020) suggests from a multi-country study that innovation capacities in the region are largely embedded in production networks with Western European MNEs and not in terms of local innovation networks. This would infer that the region lacks organic innovative capability in the face of the pandemic and this factor may perhaps determine the nature of response by less innovatively oriented SMEs.

Given the pandemic has already established a semblance of permanence in socio-economic terms, the preceding narrative serves to address resilience based responses of Hungarian SMEs upon its initial emergence and their adaptability after the first lockdown as outlined in the following research questions:-

RQ1. *How did Hungarian SMEs exhibit resilience to the pandemic when it emerged?*

RQ2. *How have Hungarian SMEs adapted to the pandemic as it has evolved in terms of resource deployment and marketing of products and services?*

4. Data Collection

A purposive sampling approach (Guest, Bunce and Johnson, 2006) was applied whereby key SMEs respondents were identified from different industrial sectors in Hungary. SMEs were selected for investigation primarily on the basis of being legally based in Hungary and employing less than 250 personnel as defined by the European Union (European Commission, 2015). A multi-sector approach was correspondingly adopted to assess how status in different industrial sectors may affect organisational resilience with cognisance of an increasingly blurred distinction between service and manufacturing oriented firms in an overall context of increased IT-orientation (Celuch and Murphy, 2010). Interviewees were in most cases CEOs which provided for comprehensive appraisal of research questions through divulgence of their knowledge and wider intuition. A total of 22 online recorded interviews were conducted in October 2020. The following table provides descriptive data of the interviewees and firms:

Table One – Descriptive Data

Interviewee	Position	No. of Employees	Industry	Supplies from abroad	Markets abroad	Year of Foundation
F1	CEO	12	Fast Food Restaurant	Y	N	2008
F2	CFO	38	Light Manufacturing	Y	Y	2006
F3	CEO	30	Translation services	Y	Y	1999
F4	CEO	10	Fintech/Personal Finance	N	Y	2017
F5	CEO	14	Language Education	N	N	1996
F6	CEO	25	IT/Online marketing	Y	Y	2009
F7	CEO	14	Light manufacturing	Y	Y	2009
F8	CEO	107	Construction	N	N	2009
F9	CEO	21	IT/Server hosting	Y	N	2014
F10	CEO	101	Passenger Transport	N	N	1994
F11	CEO	23	IT/Software Development	N	Y	2008
F12	COO	125	IT/Strategic Consulting	N	Y	2010
F13	CEO	40	IT/Data Analysis	N	Y	2012
F14	CEO	5	Wholesale/Beverages	Y	Y	2014
F15	CEO	110	Freight Transport	Y	Y	2006
F16	CEO	36	IT/Data Security	N	Y	2014
F17	CEO	11	Fintech/Salary Services	N	N	2019
F18	CEO	10	Engineering/3D Printing	Y	N	2015
F19	COO	18	Light Manufacturing	Y	Y	2017
F20	CTO	40	Light Manufacturing	Y	N	1995
F21	CEO	10	BTL marketing	Y	Y	1999
F22	CEO	8	IT/Unattended Retail	Y	Y	2016

Interviewees were asked to specifically describe their industrial sector with the majority identifying their firms as service oriented. Most firms within this category self-identified as IT businesses with two firms operating as financial technology (Fintech) entities. Firm 21 works in the 'below the line' (BTL) marketing sector, while interviewee F22 defined his enterprise as 'unattended retail' in reference to payment systems without human contact. Of the four firms defined as 'light manufacturing', F2 produces transformer devices, F7 netting material, F19 laboratory equipment and F20 industrial containers.

While the sample provides adequate variation in terms of industrial sectors, a picture of moderate international orientation is presented in that slightly less than half the sampled firms received supplies from abroad with a marginally greater proportion serving markets abroad. With nine of the firms over ten years old, the majority have relatively mature status.

5. Methodology

With the onus of this study on organisational resilience, research in this area has been largely conceptual to this point (Darkow, 2019, Hillman and Guenther, 2021) and interestingly with no specific focus on SMEs. The continuous nature of the pandemic presents opportunities for research application in that with no apparent substantial abatement of it in Hungary, organisational resilience of SMEs is also assumed to evolve in response given general uncertainty as to its duration. Hence the qualitative approach applied here focuses on generating new knowledge acquired by SME key informants.

This rationale is integral to the grounded research approach (Corbin and Strauss, 2014) whereby non-numerable data is collected and assessed through analysis of text to thereby identify emergent concepts or ideas which are then 'openly codified' and grouped into categories. In this study codes are organized in terms of findings as such categories. Higher level categories are then further inductively derived through a further open coding process involving textual examination to derive themes which forms the conceptual basis of the subsequent resilience adaption model.

Grounded research methodology is also complementary to a process oriented approach in entrepreneurship research to evaluate temporal changes in environmental phenomena (McMullen and Dimov, 2013) embodied in the pandemic. By interviewing key informants in different industrial sectors a multiple case study approach (Eisenhardt, 1989, Yin, 2017) was correspondingly applied to enhance comparison of response between key respondents given their respective sectoral contexts. A total of six open questions were devised for semi-structured interviews:

1. *Can you describe the strategies your firm used to respond to the pandemic when it began?*
2. *Can you describe the overall impact of the pandemic in terms of disruption of supplies of raw materials, labour and IT infrastructure?*
3. *What has been the effect of the pandemic until now on markets for your products or services?*
4. *How has your firm adapted to the changed situation up until now?*
5. *What has your firm learnt from the initial response to the pandemic in terms of being prepared for any future Covid-19 related events?*
6. *Do you see opportunities for adaptation of existing products and services and the introduction of new ones because of the pandemic?*

Using rationale set out by Darkow (2019) and by Kraus *et al* (2020) the first four questions were designed to assess organisational resilience based response in the formative phase of the pandemic. The two latter questions were designed to assess overall longer term adaption.

Response narrative was compared between authors to form iterative identification of recurring phrases to enable operation of the coding process of organisation into findings.

Data analysis began following each interview until it was decided that beyond a 'saturation point' further interviews would not yield unique insights (Guest, Bunce and Johnson, 2006) as broadly similar information was repeated and therefore became redundant. All interviews lasted around 30–40 minutes and were recorded and transcribed with twelve conducted in Hungarian and the remainder in English. Hungarian transcripts were translated into English and then 'back translated' (Brislin, 1970) to identify lingual inconsistencies. This preceded the previously outlined open coding process whereby areas of commonality in narrative were identified and categorized as findings.

6. Findings

The respective category titles denote open codes through identification of broadly similar narrative from all respondents whereby textual examination has resulted in categorization of common findings. Interviewees are denoted by the prefix 'F' in relation to their status in Table One.

i. Initial strategic response to the pandemic varied.

The arrival of the pandemic in Hungary was largely unanticipated although news of the virus in China in early 2020 provided sufficient time for planning. F3 (Translation services) described the initial response as *'ad hoc'* and F12 (IT consulting) admitted a *'shock effect which no one expected'*. Generally, plans were quickly formed and implemented which mostly entailed a move to homeworking whenever feasible as in the case of IT focused firms. F8 as a construction firm however 'furloughed' employees aged over 65 deemed to be at risk. Contrary to expectations structured responses were not related to firm age and size and applied to eleven firms (F2, F4, F7, F8, F9, F11, F12, E13, F16, F20, F21) in accordance with rationale outlined by Darkow (2019) in that anticipatory planning in early 2020 may have augmented resilience building capabilities. The remainder (F1, F3, F5, F6, F10, F14, F15, F17, F18, F19, F22) tended to deploy *ad hoc* responses to events as they emerged, thereby adopting continual adaption strategies from the outset.

ii. Exposure to pandemic-related economic volatility is more related to demand than supply.

F1 as a fast food provider reported a *'lack of demand but no problem with supply'*. F14, dealing in soft drink manufacturing and wholesale supply of its own product, cited a *'disastrous demand decline of 40–50 per cent'* at the beginning of the summer season. Contrary to expectations, light manufacturing firms were not severely impacted by supply chain disruptions in the early crisis phase. F2 for example reported *'diversion of supplies from China to Slovakia'*. Several IT firms, notably F4, F6, F11, F12, F13 and F22, reported cancellation or delay in projects by multi-national (MNE) clients. F21 suggested *'MNE client decision making is slower and management is more careful due to unreliable markets'*. Thus it would appear that demand related uncertainty affected SME operations to a greater degree than supply chain disruption.

iii. Virtual working has not adversely affected staff morale as the pandemic has progressed.

A shift to virtual working was least pronounced in light manufacturing and transport firms where physical presence is necessary. As expected, IT focused enterprises mostly entirely shifted operations online with some allowing restricted return to office working when the first lockdown ended but some re-curtailed access as the second wave emerged. F13 for instance allowed no more than 30 per cent of staff to work in the office.

This has morale implications in that some interviewees (F3, F9, F11, F13, F16) noted employee frustration with curtailment of personal contact. F11 suggested *'morale is good but has worsened with time'*. Some firms have HR departments (F12, F13, F16) monitoring employee well-being mostly from a health related perspective by ensuring social distancing measures were maintained. Virtual working largely continued as employees tended to be very conscious of infection risks although for IT firms this practice largely preceded the pandemic. F5, dealing in adult language education needed to deliver classes online which entailed *'drastic adaption by contracted teachers'*. Generally, it may be argued that intrinsic needs of staff to maintain employment status in the pandemic have enhanced resilience and thus may be embodied in longer term cognitive adaption.

iv. Hiring of new staff is easier than before the pandemic

This was arguably due to tightened border controls and quarantine restrictions restricting international mobility and thus increasing domestic labor supplies in Hungary. EU membership since 2004 has entailed access to more developed employment markets and a marked outflow of human capital in the CEE region (Petersen and Puliga, 2017). This aspect was noted by F10 (employee transport) *whereby 'more qualified drivers were hired as they could not drive abroad'*. Moreover, greater availability of skilled IT personnel due to pandemic related redundancy from MNEs was cited by F4, F12 and F16 as a prime reason for hiring new staff. This would again infer a cumulative effect in terms of MNE retrenchment based cost reduction measures.

v. Leadership roles of CEOs have assumed greater importance.

Interviewees were CEO/founders in 13 cases (F1, F3, F4, F6, F7, F8, F9, F13, F14, F16, F18, F21, F22) thus inferring a strong degree of entrepreneurial orientation in the sample. This would moreover suggest familiarity with adversity may drive organisational resilience as suggested by Hillman and Guenther (2021). While unpredictability through competition may be expected in 'normal' conditions, F19 suggested *'the leadership role of the CEO is of great importance in the pandemic just to motivate staff to persevere'*.

No substantial pandemic related redundancies were reported by interviewees and in general a tendency to calmly reassure staff was evident. F13 particularly emphasised this aspect while F7 stated his *'knowledge of the company's finances is indispensable'* and has no replacement. While this may infer a lack of delegation in this case, generally a semblance of collegiate decision-making was discerned to varying degrees of structure and to thus emphasise pivotal leadership roles of CEO/founders.

vi. Revenue shortfalls in given client sectors are compensated for by increases in other sectors.

In most cases drastic overall revenue declines in the early pandemic phase were reported. However, it would seem this situation has gradually been alleviated and revenue declines do not appear to be overly associated with either domestic or international market presence. Declines may rather be more firmly associated with operational sectors of clients. For example, F4 reported revenue declines in severely affected client sectors such as tourism which were compensated for by increases in sectors such as banking and insurance which according to F4 *'are accelerating digitalisation of products/services'*.

In relation to SME strategic management, exposure to any one given sector such as tourism under pandemic conditions may drastically heighten firm vulnerability. For example, F1 (fast food) reported a change to food delivery services and F21 (BTL marketing) reported a shift to digital design services, given a *'withdrawal of demand for printed exhibition material'*. This highlights the need to diversify operational focus to ensure regularity of revenue flows.

vii. Severe liquidity problems are not related to firm age.

Use of contingency based financing did not lead to severe liquidity problems in general. Cashflow was impacted in some cases by heavily ordering supplies in the early pandemic phase and ongoing unfavourable exchange rates for imported material as reported by F8 (construction), F18 (3-D printing) and F22 (unattended retail). Drastically reduced cashflow was also confirmed by F1 (fast food), F4 (fintech), F5 (language education), F14 (wholesale beverages), F17, (fintech) and F19 (laboratory equipment), thereby inferring varying extents of vulnerability in different sectors.

F5 reported sale of premises as teaching became virtual and F14 began manufacturing products at home to save rental fees. The two fintech organisations (F4 and F17) are relatively young and while both incurred substantial revenues losses with the main product given away free in the latter case, both have received venture capital funding and plan to introduce new products in 2021 in line with *'increased digitally oriented consumer demand changes'* (F17). In other cases, severe liquidity problems might be attributed to drastic demand declines and reductions in sales activities in highly exposed sectors but these were all incurred by relatively established firms. Thus it is inferred that 'tight' cashflow management may not be necessarily related to firm age but rather to direct and indirect exposure to vulnerable sectors.

viii. Government support is limited.

Several interviewees declared that other than access to salary support and loan moratorium measures available to all enterprises they receive limited government pandemic related support. For example, F16 felt the firm's financial position was *'not precarious and other similar firms were more deserving of support'*. In two IT related cases (F4 and F13), R&D grants had been received to cover 50 per cent of salary costs given their sectors are deemed by the government to assume economic priority. The salary support scheme was also used by F5 and F10 given relatively high salary costs. Firms F18 and F20 received EU funded support for small firm investment under the locally administered

'GINOP 128' programme[1] which is however not related to pandemic relief. F1 receives partial salary payment support specifically directed at the tourism sector but feels this is *'insufficient compared with SME support offered in Western European countries'* In general, this feeling was echoed given government support is not directed at the SME sector as a whole but rather at specific economic sectors. It is nonetheless interesting that firms are generally sceptical towards governmental pandemic relief, thereby suggesting preference for reliance on intrinsic resilience capabilities.

ix. Scope for adaptation and introduction of new products/services due to accelerated economic shift to digitalisation.

IT sector interviewees in particular felt there are notable long term prospects in this regard despite ongoing uncertainty. In several cases reduced sales activity was cited as a reason to update processes and products. F12, F13, F16 and F22 also suggested stronger consumer demand for digitalised products/services. F17 moreover suggested *'digitalisation caused by the pandemic may become permanent'*. While there remains a lack of empirical evidence to this effect, managerial implications exist for SMEs in terms of adapting products/services to meet wider societal changes (Ratten, 2020). Moreover in some cases products were demonstrated to clients virtually (F18, F22) thereby indicating adaption of sales processes given restrictions in marketing on a personal basis.

x. Survival prospects are varied as the pandemic continues.

Interviews took place in October 2020 just before the 'second wave' of Covid-19 infections thus within a background of long term uncertainty. Most interviewees suggested they had learnt sufficiently from the initial pandemic impact to be prepared for a second lockdown. Nonetheless continuing global economic adversity was of major concern with F1, F4, F5, F6, F14, F17 and F19 admitting to experiencing more precarious situations than the remainder of the sample. F14 stated *'the total market may shrink but it will not kill us off'*.

While all firms demonstrated resilience capabilities, it is fair to suggest the extent and nature of resilience is strongly related to operational sectors. Virtual working in particular enabled IT focused firms to continue operations largely uninterrupted, whereas firms directly exposed to public movement restrictions such as FI (fast food) and F14 (wholesale beverages) experienced dramatic demand declines. This is notable in that greater use of virtual working may enhance adaptive resilience capabilities beyond survival levels (Conz and Magnani, 2020). Although not specifically SME related, Bonacini, Gallo and Sicchitano (2021) use an Italian-based study to suggest virtual working economi-

---

[1] https://www.palyazat.gov.hu/evaluation.

cally favours relatively IT skilled 'home-working' employees in the pandemic. to infer stronger vulnerability for SME sectors where home-working is largely infeasible.

7. Thematisation

Findings as representative of commonalities shared by all interviewees were subject to a further round of textual examination in accordance with grounded research principles (Corbin and Strauss, 2014) in order to inductively derive general themes encompassing findings emerging from the research process. Four separate themes were identified as follows:

Theme 1 – Immediate use of ad hoc 'coping' response strategies

With this theme applying to half of the sample and with no discernible relationship between it and firm age and size it might be expected that smaller firms with lower resource levels would tend to deploy survival driven 'coping' strategies (Duchek, 2020). However this also applied to larger firms as in the cases of F10 and F15 (passenger and freight transport respectively). The pandemic was largely unanticipated by sample members when it first emerged in Hungary but may differ in cognitive terms in that its immediate impact was not 'visible' and urgent responses only ensued when its wider business implications became clear.

Coping based response as evident in this theme would accord with observations made by Darkow (2019) in that resilience once a crisis has begun does not assume prior anticipation of it. Moreover, coping firms were subject to little prior knowledge of the pandemic which concurrently drove coping responses after its inception based on rationale set out by Duchek (2020) whereby prevailing assumptions of operating norms were cognitively challenged and drastically altered. This would account for the more improvisational measures made in the early pandemic phase.

Theme 2 – Immediate use of reactive response strategies

Although it might be assumed more relatively experienced managers may more readily adopt a 'reactive' or relatively structured strategic response as in the example of 'attentive interventionists' (Herbane, 2019), there appears to be no firm relationship in this study between reactivity of response and firm size or age. Nonetheless some IT firms (F12, F13, F16) had HR departments which were active in pre-pandemic plan implementation upon observation of events in China in early 2020.

While HR planning is not typically associated with SMEs, (de Kok, Uhlaner and Thurik, 2006), evidence of its use in planning in this study by IT firms would suggest an implicit need to ensure continuity of operations. Moreover, a strong strategic focus on operations infers accounting for predictable risks, which reactive response firms in the sample have addressed by diversifying client sectors to ensure even revenue flows. Furthermore, reactive response firms with one exception (F4) did not appear to be drastically impacted by the immediate pandemic impact to suggest ongoing planning is beneficial in relation to continuing pandemic induced unpredictability

Theme 3 – Demonstration of longer term innovation tendencies

Thirteen firms (F1, F3, F4, F5, F9, F11, F12, F13, F16, F17, F18, F21, F22) demonstrated innovative tendencies in that all are IT oriented and were developing innovative products before the pandemic began with two exceptions (F1 and F5) which needed to innovate very quickly as a means of survival. Considering prominent expectations of major digital changes in consumer demand patterns associated with the pandemic, no substantial empirical research has yet emerged to address such a putative shift. However, Guo *et al* (2020) use a Chinese based survey to suggest the pandemic has induced investment by SMEs in digital technology. Parallels are evident in this study in firms using the pandemic to update processes and develop existing products whereas firms not strongly demonstrating innovative tendencies may not feel an intrinsic need to innovate. In some cases (F2, F7, F19) products were felt to be singularly unique and thus did not feel a need for innovative adaption. Nonetheless, innovation may be synonymous with organisational growth deriving from cognitive and structural resilience resources (Hillman and Guenther, 2021).

While optimism regarding innovation potential was expressed by many IT related interviewees in this study, such prospects may be moderated by weak 'organic' innovation potential in the CEE region outlined by Stojcic (2020) and 'institutional inefficiency' hindering technological development (Ignatov, 2019). Although both studies are not specifically SME related, they would infer innovation potential in Hungary is largely framed by transitional history over thirty years in that convergence to Western European macro-economic norms remains somewhat dormant (Beck, 2020).

Theme 4 – Longer term reactive resilience drives continuity

Eight firms (F1, F4, F5, F6, F14, F17, F19, F22) are more heavily exposed to pandemic related uncertainty and are continually adapting on a reactive basis with reference to Duchek's (2020) organizational resilience model. Furthermore, these firms operate in a variety of sectors, thus resilience is more closely associated with non-sector related limited resource availability. Parallels with the GFC are evident in that firm survival may largely depend on stoic 'social empathy' embodied in strong entrepreneurial orientation and business model adaption (Cucculelli and Peruzzi, 2020). These traits apply to a lesser degree to the less heavily exposed firms which are nonetheless also resilient in terms of continual adaption albeit perhaps in a more structured form.

8. Discussion

With reference to emergent conceptual research on organisational resilience (ie Conz and Magnani, 2020; Duchek, 2020; Hillman and Guenther, 2021) an overall scenario of varying degrees of resilience adaptation by the sampled firms is presented. The derived themes are thus used to form a conceptual basis for the resilience adaption model in Figure One:

Figure One – Resilience Adaption Model

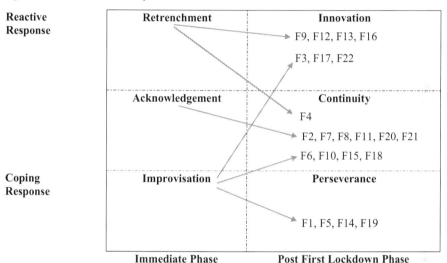

The 'immediate phase' denoted in the model includes the period from the pandemic's appearance until the end of the first lockdown (March-June 2020). The post-lockdown phase assumes longer term adaption between the end of the first and the beginning of the second lockdown (June-November, 2020).

In addition to drawing upon current organisational resilience theory, the model extends SME related work by Kraus *et al* (2020), Kuckertz *et al* (2020) and Wenzel Stanske and Lieberman (2020) in that account is made of continuous resilience driven adaption. Categories in the model are considered as resilience modes based upon Duchek's (2020) premise of using concurrent action to *cope* in the immediate aftermath of an unexpected event and using *reactive* action to reflect and learn after it has taken place with the contextual assumption that duration of the pandemic is unknown.

By building on work by Kraus *et al* (2020) and Wenzel, Stanske and Lieberman (2020), the model assumes that firms may amend resilience driven responses as the pandemic continues denoted by the direction of arrows in Figure One indicating paths to respective post-impact resilience modes of sample members. While the model does not preclude this progession as in the 'improvisation-continuity' (F6, F10, F15, F18) and 'improvisation-innovation' paths (F3, F17, F22) the majority of firms retained original coping and reactive responses into the post lockdown phase albeit by adopting different modes of resilience.

Rationale for coping responses is partially derived from research by Kuckertz *et al* (2020) whereby startup firms cope with initial adversity by adopting *improvisation* of existing resources as depicted in figure one. *Perseverance* as a resilience mode in the post lockdown phase (F1,F5,F14,F19) assumes longer term adaption survival is driven by continuing bricolage based resource utilization (Conz and Magnani, 2020). Firms following the coping based *improvisation-perseverance* path continue reactively responding and thus may be seen as more vulnerable to the pandemic and are assumed to be more concerned with survival than innovation of products and services.

Reactive response resilience modes in the immediate crisis phase of the model are differentiated as *'retrenchment'* and *'acknowledgement'* given the former category assumes pre-planned resource control measures are taken to ensure continuity of operations products/services (Herbane, 2019). Firms adopting *retrenchment* are moreover assumed to conserve resources sufficiently to pursue *innovation* in the post lockdown phase (F9, F12, F13, F16). It is notable these firms are all IT oriented thereby implying adaption of an *innovation* resilience mode may be related to the extent to which product/service modification may in turn be induced by digitally driven client demand accelerated by the pandemic (Ratten, 2020). This aspect is to a limited extent evident in for example adaption of reactive response of F17 in this study which as an IT firm may have felt a drastic need to innovate due to drastic revenue loss in the immediate phase.

'Acknowledgement' as a reactive resilience response mode is by contrast defined as cognitive acceptance of the initial pandemic impact and maintaining *continuity* of operations into the post lockdown phase following rationale set out by Hillmann and Guenther (2021). Firms following the *acknowledgement-continuity* path (F2, F7,F8, F11, F20, F21) did not perceive an overriding need to innovate products/services.

In summation of the preceding narrative, the model developed is unique in that extant literature does not reveal major focus on resilience adaption by SMEs to transboundary events (Boin, 2019) such as the current pandemic. With little empirical research conducted on SME crisis management in the CEE region before the pandemic, it can be expected that it might also assume emphasis on resilience adaption. However the existence of macro-economic decoupling between the region and Western Europe (Beck, 2020) and a lack of domestic organic innovation capabilities (Stojcic, 2020) may largely determine resilience adaption modes identified in this study. This forms a basis for addressing the research questions forthwith:

RQ1.   How did Hungarian SMEs respond strategically to the Covid 19 pandemic when it emerged?

Following rational set out by Duchek (2020) there is sufficient evidence in this study to suggest a strong degree of *anticipation* of the pandemic but there was nonetheless a sense of an 'ontological shock' (Herbane, 2019) whereby existing perceptions of environmental conditions were radically altered. Even application of coping and reactive responses in this study infers lack of uniformity unrelated to firm sector, size or age. Reactive responses may be more closely related to greater availability of resources but initial response modes have largely determined the nature of post-lockdown response. It is notable that immediate term coping responses are more closely associated with firms operating in sectors such as fast food where direct contact with customers was drastically restricted. Thus the feasibility of implementing homeworking conditions may be crucial in this regard.

RQ2.   How have Hungarian SMEs adapted to the crisis as it has evolved in terms of resource deployment and marketing of products and services?

Again with reference to Duchek's (2020) organisational resilience model, the majority of firms in this study adopted cognitively driven reactively based resilience adaption modes of continuity and innovation. Thus a process of reflection rather than reflexive reaction is evident to suggest existence of continual learning. Moreover, it is again notable that firms with greater resource levels are apparently better able to contemplate and develop innovation possibilities. Firms deemed to be 'coping' are assumed to persevere in the longer term in the hope the pandemic may recede. Furthermore there is no notable distinction between firms in terms of sectors between coping and reactive responses in the longer term. Thus exposure to drastic demand fluctuations is probably a key determining factor of response mode.

9. Conclusion

This study represents a formative attempt to address the business related effects of the Covid-19 pandemic on SMEs in the CEE region. Findings partially corroborate those of other CEE studies. For example, Chudziński *et al* (2021) derived similar conclusions with regard to homeworking policies of businesses in Poland although this study was not specifically SME related. At this point literature also reveals no firm conceptual linkage between medical and business related effects of the pandemic although Sharma *et al* (2021) use an Indian based study to suggest increased new infection rates have a direct macro-economic impact. In this regard, emergence of new Covid-19 virus variants as currently experienced in the CEE region (WHO, 2021) alongside vaccination efforts serves to heighten uncertainty of the pandemic's duration.

This has implications in terms of adapting to repeated infection waves and consequent lockdown and re-opening cycles. In this regard, findings drawn from this article provide indication of ongoing SME resilience based response in relation to the CEE transitional context whereby socio-economic and macro-economic factors may serve to heighten organisational challenges faced by SMEs in comparison with those located in more deeply embedded market economies. Moreover, the pandemic represents a dramatic departure from perceptions of crises as single events. Climatic change for example is analogous to the pandemic in this regard thereby serving to heighten a need to adopt a resilience-based approach by SMEs in the face of perennial uncertainty.

Various limitations are notable in this paper. Principally, sole use of qualitative research methods is insufficient in terms of deriving generalisations as to the effect of the pandemic on the entire SME sector. IT firms are strongly represented, thus presenting an uneven balance in terms of industrial sectors. The survey was conducted at a specific point in time following the first lockdown and ideally would have been better augmented with a subsequent wide ranging longitudinal survey. The firms surveyed were of various size, age and sector which also renders multiple possibilities for interpretation of the resilience adaption model. Moreover research was conducted in a relatively small transitional country with its own specific socio-economic characteristics. Given the global nature of the pandemic, findings are therefore not universally applicable.

Nonetheless, the resilience adaption model formed in this study may assist in terms of locating resilience modes of SMEs in need of urgent policy support. It is also notable that organisational resilience constitutes a formative area of research and there is no substantial work on its application to SMEs. Future research may thus deviate from preceding work on SME crisis management whereby reversion to a pre-crisis environment is assumed. Hence this study may act as a guide to future research efforts focusing on SME organisational resilience in response to transboundary transmitted uncertainty as embodied in the Covid-19 pandemic.

Acknowledgments

The authors would like to express their gratitude to Orsolya Szikra, MSc student at Corvinus University Budapest, for her work as research assistant in this project.

Gergely Freész's contribution was sponsored by the Sylff Association – The Tokyo Foundation for Policy Research.

References

Andor, G./Tóth, T. (2018): Non-financial Background of Success around Global Financial Crisis--Evidence from Eastern Europe, in: Facta Universitatis, Series: Economics and Organization,15, 4, 305–17.

Artner, A. (2018): Is Catching Up Possible? The Example of Central and Eastern Europe, in: Science & Society, 82, 4, 502–530.

Beck, K. (2020): Decoupling after the Crisis: Western and Eastern Business Cycles in the European Union, in: Eastern European Economics, 58,1, 68–82.

Boin, A. (2019): The Transboundary Crisis: Why we are unprepared and the road ahead, in: Journal of Contingencies & Crisis Management, 27,1, 94–99.

Bonacini, L./Gallo, G./Scicchitano, S. (2021): Working from home and income inequality: risks of a 'new normal' with COVID-19, in: Journal of Population Economics, 34, 1, 303–60.

Brislin, R.W. (1970): Back-translation for cross-cultural research, in: Journal of Cross-Cultural Psychology, 32,1,185–216.

Celuch, K./Murphy, G. (2010): SME Internet use and strategic flexibility: the moderating effect of IT market orientation, in: Journal of Marketing Management, 26, 1/2, 131–145.

Chudziński, P./Cyfert, S./Dyduch,W./ Zastempowski, M. (2021): Key sur(VIR)val factors in water supply companies: some lessons from Poland, in: Journal of Water Supply: Research and Technology-Aqua, 70,1, 89–98.

Cucculelli, M./Peruzzi,V. (2020): Post-crisis Firm Survival, Business Model Changes, and Learning: Evidence from the Italian Manufacturing Industry, in: Small Business Economics, 54, 2, 459–74.

Conz, E./Magnani, G. (2020): A dynamic perspective on the resilience of firms: A systematic literature review and a framework for future research, in: European Management Journal, 38,3, 400–412.

Corbin, J./Strauss, A. (2014): Basics of Qualitative Research: Techniques and Procedures for Developing Grounded Theory, Thousand Oaks, CA: Sage Publications.

Darkow, P.M. (2019): Beyond "bouncing back": Towards an integral, capability-based understanding of organizational resilience, in: Journal of Contingencies & Crisis Management, 27, 2, 145–156.

de Kok, J.M.P./Uhlaner, L. M./Thurik, A. R. (2006): Professional HRM Practices in Family Owned-Managed Enterprises, in: Journal of Small Business Management, 44,3, 441–460.

Doern, R./Williams, N./Vorley, T. (2019): Special issue on entrepreneurship and crises: business as usual? An introduction and review of the literature, in: Entrepreneurship & Regional Development, 31, 5/6, 400–412.

Duchek, S.(2020): Organizational resilience: a capability-based conceptualization, in: Business Research, 13,1, 215–246.

Eggers, F. (2020): Masters of disasters? Challenges and opportunities for SMEs in times of crisis, in: Journal of Business Research, 116, 199–208.

Eisenhardt, K.M. (1989): Building theories from case study research, in: Academy of Management Review, 14, 4, 532–550.

Etemad, H. (2020): Managing uncertain consequences of a global crisis: SMEs encountering adversities, losses, and new opportunities, in: Journal of International Entrepreneurship,18,2, 125–144.

European Commission (2015): User guide to the SME Definition, European Commission, Brussels,1–60. https://ec.europa.eu/regional_policy/sources/conferences/stateaid/sme/smedefinitionguide_en.pdf

European Commission (2019): SBA Factsheet Hungary, European Commission, Brussels, 2–23. AppData/Local/Temp/Hungary – SBA Fact Sheet 2019–1.pdf

European Commission (2020): Details of Hungary's support measures to help citizens and companies during the significant economic impact of the coronavirus pandemic, European Commission, Brussels, https://ec.europa.eu/info/live-work-travel-eu/health/coronavirus-response/jobs-and-economy-during-coronavirus-pandemic/state-aid-cases/hungary_en

European Commission (2021): Winter 2021 Economic Forecast, Press Release 11 February 2021, European Commission, Brussels, https://ec.europa.eu/commission/presscorner/detail/en/ip_21_504

Eurostat (2021): Euroindicators, GDP news release, 9 March 2021, https://ec.europa.eu/eurostat/documents/2995521/11562975/2-09032021-AP-EN.pdf/2cf0fd87-a11d-a0eb-ca36-2092f1574f80?t=1615239292163

Freeman, J./Carroll, G.R./Hannan, M.T. (1983): The liability of newness: Age dependence in organizational death rates, in: American Sociological Review, 48, 5, 692–710.

Guest, G./Bunce, A./Johnson, L. (2006): How many interviews are enough? An experiment with data saturation and variability, in : Field Methods,18, 1, 59–82.

Guo, H./Yang, Z./Huang, R./Guo, A. (2020): The digitalization and public crisis responses of small and medium enterprises: Implications from a COVID-19 survey, in: Frontiers of Business Research in China,14,1, 1–25.

Herbane, B. (2019): Rethinking Organizational Resilience and Strategic Renewal in SMEs, in: Entrepreneurship and Regional Development, 31, 5–6, 476–95.

Hillmann, J./Guenther, E.(2021): Organizational Resilience: A Valuable Construct for Management Research? in: International Journal of Management Reviews, 23,1, 7–44.

Hungarian Central Statistical Office (2021): Weekly Monitor, 30 March 2021, Hungarian Central Statistical Office (Központi Statisztikai Hivatal), Budapest, Hungary, http://www.ksh.hu/?lang=en

Ignatov, A. (2019): Institutional efficiency, entrepreneurship, and the premises of economic development in the Eastern European countries, in: Studia Universitatis Babes-Bolyai, Geology, 64, 2, 12–32.

Karácsony, P. (2020):The impact of the Coronavirus (Covid-19) on the employment characteristics of Hungarian SMEs, in: Review of Economic Studies & Research Virgil Madgearu, 13, 2, 1–4.

Kim, K. /Yoon, H.Y. /Jung, K. (2017): Resilience in risk communication networks: Following the 2015 MERS response in South Korea, in: Journal of Contingencies & Crisis Management, 25, 3, 148–159.

Kraus, S./Clauß, T./Breier, M./Gast, J./Zardini, A./Tiberius, V. (2020): The economics of COVID-19: Initial empirical evidence on how family firms in five European countries cope with the corona crisis, in: International Journal of Entrepreneurial Behaviour & Research, 26, 5, 1067–1092.

Kuckertz, A./Brändle, L./Gaudig, A./Hinderer, S./Morales Reyes, C.A./Prochotta, A./Steinbrink, K.M./Berger, E.S.C. (2020): Startups in times of crisis – A rapid response to the COVID-19 pandemic, in: Journal of Business Venturing Insights, 13, e00169, 1–13.

Lee, J.W./McKibbin, W.J. (2004): Globalization and disease: the case of SARS, in: Asian Economic Papers, 3, 1, 113–131.

McMullen, J.S./Dimov, D. (2013): Time and the Entrepreneurial Journey: The Problems and Promise of Studying Entrepreneurship as a Process, in: Journal of Management Studies, 50, 8,1481–1512.

Petersen, A. M./Puliga, M. (2017): High-skilled labour mobility in Europe before and after the 2004 enlargement, in: Journal of the Royal Society Interface, 14,128, 1–13.

Ratten, V. (2020): Coronavirus and international business: An entrepreneurial ecosystem perspective in: Thunderbird International Business Review, 62, 5, 629–634.

Sharma, G.D./ Tiwari, A.K./ Jain, M./ Yadav, A./ Erkut, B. (2021): Unconditional and conditional analysis between covid-19 cases, temperature, exchange rate and stock markets using wavelet coherence and wavelet partial coherence approaches, in: Heliyon, 7, 2, 1–30.

Stojčić, N. (2020): Collaborative innovation in emerging innovation systems: Evidence from Central and Eastern Europe, in: The Journal of Technology Transfer, 46, 2, 531–562.

Wenzel, M./Stanske, S./Lieberman, M.B. (2020): Strategic responses to crisis, in: Strategic Management Journal, 41, V7–V18.

World Bank (2019): Hungary Trade Statistics, World Bank, Washington, USA. https://wits.worldbank.org/CountryProfile/en/HUN

World Health Organization (2020): Novel coronavirus (2019-nCoV) SITUATION REPORT – 209, August 16 2020, Novel Coronavirus: World Health Organization, Geneva. https://www.who.int/docs/default-source/coronaviruse/situation-reports/20200816-covid-19-sitrep-209.pdf?sfvrsn=5dde1ca2_2

World Health Organization (2021): Coronavirus disease (Covid-19) Weekly Epidemiological Update, April 6 2021, World Health Organization, Geneva. https://www.who.int/publications/m/item/weekly-epidemiological-update-on-covid-19---6-april-2021

Welter, F./Smallbone, D.(2011): Institutional Perspectives on Entrepreneurial Behavior in Challenging Environments, in : Journal of Small Business Management, 49,1, 107–125.

Wildavsky, A. B. (2004): Searching for safety New Brunswick, London: Transaction Publishers. 3rd Edition.

Yin, R.K. (2017): Case Study Research: Design and Methods. Thousand Oaks, CA: Sage Publications, 6th edition.

COVID-19 implications on the Polish stock market – the sector indices level[*]

Bogna Kaźmierska-Jóźwiak, Paweł Sekuła, Błażej Socha[**]

Abstract

The main aim of the study is to investigate the Polish stock market reaction to COVID-19. Using event-study methodology we investigate the impact of two COVID-19 events that represent the influence of shock and stimulus on the sector indices reaction on the Warsaw Stock Exchange (WSE). The first event day is March 11, 2020 when the World Health Organisation (WHO) declared the COVID-19 outbreak as a pandemic. The second event is April 9, 2020 when the Federal Reserve Bank (FED) announced the largest stimulus package in history worth up to $2.3 trillion. In order to examine the stock market reaction, we use event study methodology and analyse the abnormal return (AR) and cumulative abnormal return (CAR) calculated on the basis of the market model. We confirm a heterogeneous effect of the COVID-19 pandemic outbreak and the FED stimulus package announcement on sector (indices) of the WSE.

Keywords: COVID-19, financial market, company, Warsaw Stock Exchange, event study methodology, sector indices
JEL Codes: G01, G14, M21

Introduction

The outbreak of the COVID-19 pandemic has affected people all over the world. It has had far-reaching consequences beyond the spread itself. Countries responded by locking down people and business activity as well as implementing stimulus packages to weaken the devastating slowdown in economic activity.

The impact of the current pandemic on various areas of the economy of a given country has recently been thoroughly studied around the world. The capital market is a very important part of the economy and, as assumed, the capital market's reaction to the COVID-19 pandemic has attracted the interest of researchers all over the world (Al-Awadhi/Alsaifi/Al-Awadhi/Alhamadi 2020; Ali/Alam/Rizvi 2020; Baker/Bloom/Davis/Kost/Sammon/Viratyosin 2020; Czech/Wielechowski/Kotyza/Benešová/Laputková 2020; Mazur/Dang/Vega 2020; Narayan/Devpura/Hua 2020; Phan/Narayan 2020; Zhang/Hu/Ji 2020).

---

[*] Received: 31.12.20, Accepted: 28.10.21, 2 revisions.
[**] *Bogna Kaźmierska-Jóźwiak* (Corresponding author), Ph.D., Assistant Professor, Faculty of Management, University of Lodz, Poland. Email: bogna.kazmierska@uni.lodz.pl. Main research interest: corporate finance, dividend policy, mergers and acquisitions.
Paweł Sekuła, Ph.D., Assistant Professor, Faculty of Management, University of Lodz, Poland. Email: pawel.sekula@uni.lodz.pl. Main research interest: corporate finance, market efficiency, behavioral finance.
Błażej Socha, Ph.D., Assistant Professor, Faculty of Management, University of Lodz, Poland. Email: blazej.socha@uni.lodz.pl. Main research interest: financing decisions and corporate governance in family business, corporate finance.

The authors of this study analysed the stock market reaction to two events that represent the shock and the stimulus. Following Harjoto/Rossi/Paglia (2020 b) the market reaction to the following events were examined: the WHO announcement of the pandemic on March 11, 2020 and the Federal Reserve Bank announcement on April 9, 2020 regarding the largest stimulus package in history worth up to $2.3 trillion. This decision could have an impact on the world financial markets, taking into consideration the importance of the US economy.

The main aim of the study is to investigate the effect of COVID-19 on the stock market reaction, analysing the sector indices of the Warsaw Stock Exchange.

Therefore, the following research questions have been formulated:

RQ (1): How do sector indices of the WSE react to the information announced by the WHO regarding the COVID-19 pandemic outbreak?

RQ (2): How do sector indices of the WSE react to the information regarding the stimulus action undertaken in the US?

Following the literature (Alam/Wei/Wahid 2020; Ramelli/Wagner 2020; Mazur/Dang/Vega 2021; Narayan/Gong/Ali Ahmed 2021; Akhtaruzzaman/Boubaker/Sensoy 2021), it is hypothesised that COVID-19 has had a heterogenous effect on the Polish stock market.

This study makes several contributions. First of all, the authors focus on the Polish stock exchange market – the largest stock exchange in Central Eastern Europe. Taking into consideration the number of equities listed on the Prague Stock Exchange (PSE – 10 equities on the Prime Market), the Bratislava Stock Exchange (BSSE – 2 equities on the Main Market), or the Budapest Stock Exchange (BSE – 40 equities), and the fact that the above-mentioned stock exchanges do not publish sector indices, it is not possible to conduct the research on sector indices there. The WSE is the only stock exchange in Central Eastern Europe on which the sector indices analysis is possible.

Secondly, the authors examine COVID-19 implications on the sector indices. There are several studies analysing COVID-19 implications on the Polish stock market among other stock markets (i.a. Czech et al. 2020; Ashraf 2020; Ding/Levine/Lin/Xie 2021), but none focuses on the indices level. In this study, the decision was made to consider not the entire Polish stock market (main index of the Warsaw Stock Exchange), but the sector indices. It is assumed that some sectors become highly vulnerable while others continue to perform well even in the crisis period, caused by COVID-19. To the best of the authors' knowledge, this research is the first attempt to analyse the COVID-19 implications on the sector indices on the WSE.

Following Alam et al. (2020), Narayan et al. (2021), Ramelli and Wagner (2020) and Mazur et al. (2021), the stock market reaction to the COVID-19 events is analysed using the sector's indices to examine the industry reaction to COVID-19. Following the study of Harjoto et al. (2020 b) an investigation is made into the stock market reactions to the shock: the WHO announcement of the COVID-19 outbreak as a pandemic and the stimulus – the announcement of the Federal Reserve Bank's largest stimulus package in history worth up to $2.3 trillion. This decision could have an impact on world financial markets, taking into consideration the importance of the US economy. The authors' aim is to check how the Polish stock market indices are sensitive to the particular COVID-19 events.

Regarding the above-mentioned data and elaborated in the next section literature background, which showed that the reaction to shock varies depending on the economic conditions of a given country and market, it is important to examine the COVID-19 pandemic implications on the Central Eastern European economy and its capital markets. The results of the study could be interesting for investors, companies and also for the governments to understand the COVID-19 implications on different sector indices and to plan the recovery action for the companies from different sectors in order to enable investors to recover their confidence to make investment decisions.

This paper is organised as follows. Section 2 reviews the literature. Section 3 describes the methodology and data. Section 4 presents the research results and the discussion. The conclusions are presented in the last section.

Literature review

It should be noted that the COVID-19 outbreak was exceptional in many ways – by the extreme scope, level and uncertainty. For the first time in history so many countries all over the world decided to lock down their economies. This is the primary reason why the shock triggered by COVID-19 is different from other shocks. As Roubini (2020) argues "the shock to the global economy from Covid-19 has been faster and more severe than the 2008 global financial crisis and even the Great Depression". The pandemic has hit business all around the world in an unprecedented scale and speed. It has caused disruption to manufacturing industries and their supply chains. The pandemic has already impacted the supply chain on a large scale. The World Economic Forum highlighted the need for firms to reengineer and adapt supply chains to their future trade challenges (WEF 2020).

Studies examining the impact of COVID-19 on stock market performance have emerged quickly over the past year. There has been quite a lot of literature focusing on the US (Baker et al. 2020; Ramelli/Wagner 2020; Harjoto et al. 2020 b; Chen/Yeh 2021; Mazur et al. 2021), Australia (Alam et al. 2020;

Narayan et al. 2021; Rahman/Amin/Al Mamun 2021), China (Al-Awadhi et al. 2020; Yan 2020; Xiong/WU/Hou/Zhang 2020; Akhtaruzzaman et al. 2021).

There are also studies investigating the COVID-19 implications on the financial markets comparing the international data. Zhang et al. (2020) explore the patterns of global financial markets reactions (i.a. US, UK, China, Spain, Germany, France, Japan, Singapore). Cao, Li and Woo (2020) focus on the 14 market indices from Asia (China, Hong Kong, Taiwan, Singapore, Japan, South Korea), Europe (Germany, the UK, France, Spain, Italy), North America (US, Canada) and Australia. Akhtaruzzaman et al. (2021) examine how financial contagion occurs through financial and nonfinancial firms between China and G7 countries during the COVID-19 period. Harjoto, Rossi, Lee and Kownatzki (2020 a) evaluate the impact of the COVID-19 on the financial stock markets across emerging and developed countries (a sample consists of 76 countries). Emerging markets were the topic of the study conducted by Topcu and Gulal (2020). Liu, Manzoor, Wang, Zhang and Manzoor (2020) examine the short-term impact of the coronavirus outbreak on 21 leading stock market indices in major affected countries (including the US, Japan, Korea, Singapore, Germany, Italy, the UK etc). Espinoza-Mendez and Arias (2021) focus on financial markets from Italy, Germany, the UK and Spain as the first countries that reported COVID-19 in Europe. The authors examine whether COVID-19 had an effect on herding behaviour in Europe (over the period from January 03, 2000 to June 19, 2020). Czech et al. (2020) examine the short-term reaction of the financial markets in the Visegrad countries (the Czech Republic, Hungary, Poland and Slovakia) to the COVID-19 pandemic. Heyden and Heyden (2021) study the short-term market reactions of US and European stocks during the beginning of the COVID-19 pandemic. The study findings suggest that stock markets react differently to the announcement of the first case and the first death in the country. Moreover, the stock markets react negatively to the announcements of country-specific fiscal policy measures, however, the monetary policy measures have the potential to calm markets.

This study's work is related to studies that have examined the effect of COVID-19 on the stock market reaction and to evaluate the sector performance. Alam et al. (2020) use event study methodology to examine the impact of COVID-19 on eight selected industries in Australia. Firstly, the study results show that some industry indices are sensitive to the official announcement of the pandemic in Australia. On February 27, 2020, the day the COVID-19 pandemic was announced in Australia, there are three sectors – food, pharmaceuticals and healthcare – which earn a positive statistically significant abnormal return. Secondly, the findings confirm a great variation among the sectors.

He, Sun, Zhang and Li (2020) investigate the impact of COVID-19 on the stock prices of Chinese industries. The findings show that the pandemic negatively impacted stock prices on the Shanghai Stock Exchange, whereas positively on the Shenzhen Stock Exchange. COVID-19 negatively affected the traditional industries of China (i.a. the transportation, mining, electric and heating, and environmental industries). However, the manufacturing, information technology, education, and health industries positively responded to COVID-19.

Ramelli and Wagner (2020) provide evidence of heterogeneous impacts of the pandemic on the US stock returns across industries. Based on the study results they suggest that firms from the consumer services sector were the biggest losers, food and staples retailers were among the strongest winners over the period called Fever (Monday, February 24 through to Friday, March 20).

Narayan et al. (2021) focus on the Australian stock market, evaluating how COVID-19 has impacted on eleven different sectors. They argue that the pandemic has had a heterogeneous effect on sectors of the market, with sectors such as health, information technology and consumer staples gaining. They claim that this type of asymmetric effect is caused by the fact that during COVID-19, particular firms (such as healthcare, consumer staples and information technology) have benefitted, while others (such as communication, energy, finance, and consumer discretion) have lost the advantage.

Mazur et al. (2021) investigate single-day extreme events (Black Monday, Black Thursday, and Black Monday II) on the S&P 1500 firms. Due to the results, the authors claim that in some sectors stocks earn positive returns (i.a. natural gas, food, healthcare, and software), whereas other sectors fall dramatically (petroleum, real estate, entertainment, and hospitality sectors). Moreover, the findings show a differential reaction to COVID-19 for firms in the same sector. Stock price crashes lead to extreme volatility.

Chen and Yeh (2021) use data of companies listed on the NYSE, AMEX, or NASDAQ and form 49 industry portfolios. The study examines industrial reactions to the COVID-19 pandemic, compared to the reaction to the global financial crisis of 2008. The findings confirm that most industries in the US suffered from both events, however, most industries started to recover after the announcements of quantitative easing. The effect of quantitative easing in 2020 on stock performance is more significant for the industries that are more affected by COVID-19. The authors argue that the quantitative easing is an effective method in boosting investor confidence.

Research methodology

Following Alam et al. (2020), Narayan et al. (2021), Ramelli and Wagner (2020) and Mazur et al. (2021), the stock market reaction to the COVID-19 events is examined using the sector's indices. Event study may reveal how the sector indices of the stock market could be sensitive to a particular event. Following the study of Harjoto et al. (2020 b) the stock market reactions to the shock is investigated: the WHO announcement of the COVID-19 outbreak as a pandemic, and the stimulus – the announcement of the Federal Reserve Bank largest stimulus package in history worth up to $2.3 trillion. This decision could have an impact on world financial markets, taking into consideration the importance of the US economy. This study's aim is to examine how the sector indices of the Polish stock market are sensitive to particular COVID-19 events.

The paper focuses on the sector indices calculated by the Warsaw Stock Exchange: WIG-automobiles&parts, WIG-banking, WIG-chemical, WIG-construction, WIG-clothes (includes companies from the clothing & cosmetics sector), WIG-energy, WIG-food (includes companies from the food and drinks sector), WIG-games (includes companies from the game developers sector), WIG-IT, WIG-media, WIG-mining, WIG-oil&gas, WIG-real estate, WIG-pharmaceuticals, WIG-telecom.

As research methodology an event study is used, which mainly examines the abnormal returns of a security price after a specific event occurs (Brown and Warner, 1980). In this paper the event study is used to examine the impact of the COVID-19 pandemic on the stock market.

The research sample consists of 15 sector-indices of the Warsaw Stock Exchange. Rates of returns were calculated on the basis of the closing values of each index. Data was retrieved from the Warsaw Stock Exchange database.

In applying the event study methodology (Brown and Warner, 1985), two event days were identified:

– March 11, 2020 – which represents the shock caused by the WHO announcement,
– April 9, 2020 – which relates to the stimulus action announced by the FED.

The event period was comprised of 11 days (11-day window, providing -5/+5 days around the event day) and 21 days (21-day window, providing -10/+10 days around the event day).

To measure market reaction abnormal return (AR) and cumulative abnormal return (CAR) were calculated. The first step was to calculate the daily rates of return for sector indices as well as the market index. The rates of return for all sector indices of the WSE were determined.

The abnormal returns were computed using a market model (Brown and Warner, 1985):

$$AR_{i,t} = R_{i,t} - \left(\hat{\alpha}_i + \hat{\beta}_i R_{m,t}\right) \tag{1}$$

Where:

$AR_{i,t}$ – the abnormal return on the i-sector index for day t,

$R_{i,t}$ – the return on the i-sector index for day t,

$R_{m,t}$ – the return on the market index for day t,

Alfa $(\hat{\alpha}_i)$ and beta $(\hat{\beta}_i)$ parameters were estimated based on the data from the estimation period. The classical least squares regression (CLS) was used. If the assumptions of CLS were not met, the generalised least squares regression (GLS) was used.

For each index 250 daily rates of return observations were used (Brown and Warner, 1985), which covered the estimation period and the event period. Hence, for the 11-day window an estimation window of 239 trading days (from -244 to -6) was used, for the 21-day window an estimation window consisted of 229 trading days (from -239 to -11).

The cumulative abnormal returns on the i-sector index in (t_1, t_2) time window were calculated using the following formula:

$$CAR_i(t_1, t_2) = \sum_{t=t_1}^{t_2} AR_{it} \qquad (2)$$

where:

AR – abnormal return for i-sector index in (t_1, t_2) time window.

In order to test the significance of the results, a test based on the *t*-statistic was applied (Alam et al. 2020).

Results and discussion

In this section, the results of research for the two identified event days are presented. Firstly, the parametric tests results for the ARs around both events (in a chronological order) in an 11-day window are presented. Then the parametric tests results for the CARs around both events for the 11 and 21-day window. Additionally, the presentation of how the cumulative abnormal returns change over time (from day -5 to day 5). The discussion is conducted in relation to the prior studies.

Table 1. ARs – the WHO announcement (March 11, 2020)

Event period day	AR	t-ratio	AR	t-ratio	AR	t-ratio
	WIG-banking		WIG-construction		WIG-chemical	
-5	0.35	0.6263	0.24	0.2612	0.64	0.4471
-4	-0.26	0.4592	-0.36	0.3856	-1.37	0.9602
-3	-0.26	0.4536	0.80	0.8636	2.17	1.5136
-2	-0.80	1.4160	-2.43	2.6255***	-0.30	0.2073
-1	0.16	0.2893	1.52	1.6417	0.25	0.1727
0	**0.51**	**0.9085**	**-1.30**	**1.4064**	**-1.80**	**1.2559**
+1	-1.28	2.2830**	-0.46	0.4957	1.70	1.1873
+2	-0.10	0.1778	-1.45	1.5618	-2.47	1.7279*
+3	-6.56	11.6776***	-3.34	3.6042***	1.54	1.0780
+4	-0.49	0.8779	-1.82	1.9671*	4.91	3.4322***
+5	-1.35	2.4081**	0.28	0.3064	6.34	4.4337***
	WIG-energy		WIG-games		WIG-mining	
-5	-0.67	0.4489	-1.36	0.8971	-0.76	0.5644
-4	-0.75	0.5130	1.28	0.8458	-0.46	0.3463
-3	-0.54	0.3696	0.38	0.2509	0.63	0.4707
-2	1.86	1.2687	-1.81	1.1947	1.61	1.2045
-1	0.08	0.0536	-0.29	0.1918	1.96	1.4679
0	**-0.27**	**0.1862**	**-1.88**	**1.2404**	**3.52**	**2.6336***
+1	-0.84	0.5711	-6.25	4.1228***	5.39	4.0277***
+2	-2.23	1.5251	5.05	3.3275***	-0.12	0.0883
+3	4.61	3.1536***	11.33	7.4721***	3.39	2.5316**
+4	5.32	3.6390***	0.18	0.1154	-1.80	1.3447
+5	3.78	2.5864**	0.04	0.0265	-1.77	1.3251
	WIG-IT		WIG-pharmaceuticals		WIG-media	
-5	0.30	0.3007	0.44	0.2328	2.91	2.5307**
-4	0.21	0.2106	-0.09	0.0500	0.42	0.3617
-3	0.24	0.2387	-2.19	1.1659	-5.48	4.7620***
-2	-1.68	1.6740*	-10.93	5.8298***	-4.67	4.0564***
-1	0.28	0.2803	-2.51	1.3376	1.61	1.3989
0	**0.17**	**0.1729**	**-5.20**	**2.7705***	**-3.89**	**3.3836***
+1	-0.85	0.8455	-10.59	5.6485***	-4.36	3.7938***
+2	2.43	2.4179**	6.50	3.4691***	-10.43	9.0670***
+3	0.60	0.5958	13.77	7.3444***	-4.72	4.1075***
+4	0.02	0.0229	12.39	6.6084***	6.42	5.5811***
+5	-1.96	1.9536*	-4.83	2.5770**	1.20	1.0403

Event period day	AR	t-ratio	AR	t-ratio	AR	t-ratio
	WIG-automobiles&parts		WIG-real estate		WIG-clothes	
-5	-0.82	0.7987	0.47	0.6895	-0.13	0.1063
-4	-0.77	0.7493	0.75	1.0956	-0.33	0.2781
-3	-1.41	1.3745	0.65	0.9524	0.06	0.0483
-2	-2.52	2.4552**	-4.13	6.0222***	-0.53	0.4463
-1	0.25	0.2444	2.68	3.9074***	-1.52	1.2787
0	-1.96	1.9116*	-1.05	1.5348	-2.10	1.7680**
+1	-8.28	8.0681***	-0.31	0.4527	-2.07	1.7385**
+2	-1.86	1.8116*	-1.46	2.1319**	-4.10	3.4429***
+3	-3.82	3.7244***	-2.45	3.5741***	-7.03	5.9087***
+4	0.19	0.1836	-0.78	1.1376	3.41	2.8636***
+5	1.91	1.8611*	-3.71	5.4051***	-4.32	3.6297***
	WIG-oil&gas		WIG-food		WIG-telecom	
-5	-2.01	1.7548*	-1.69	1.8717*	2.40	1.7749*
-4	-1.56	1.3673	1.19	1.3148	-0.28	0.2047
-3	-1.54	1.3489	-1.37	1.5219	2.07	1.5331
-2	6.42	5.6220***	-3.34	3.7112***	0.27	0.1981
-1	-2.24	1.9639*	0.98	1.0910	-2.55	1.8872*
0	-1.95	1.7029*	-0.92	1.0164	2.43	1.8004*
+1	8.40	7.3517***	-5.88	6.5253***	0.89	0.6583
+2	1.38	1.2078	9.60	10.6484***	-4.81	3.5650***
+3	6.65	5.8204***	-6.77	7.5133***	8.06	5.9689***
+4	-4.43	3.8819***	-0.19	0.2095	2.83	2.0975**
+5	0.32	0.2835	-0.80	0.8868	2.00	1.4834

***, **, * significant at 1 %, 5 %, 10 % respectively
Source: author's own elaboration.

Due to the study results (see Table 1), the WHO announcement created negative and statistically significant abnormal returns for five indices (WIG-pharmaceuticals, WIG-oil&gas, WIG-clothes, WIG-automobiles&parts, WIG-media). In the case of six other indices, negative abnormal returns can be observed, however, the results are not statistically significant. Surprisingly, the first (shock) event is associated with positive statistically significant abnormal returns for two indices (WIG-telecom, WIG-mining), for two others the positive reaction is not statistically significant.

The study's findings confirm that WIG-pharmaceuticals, WIG-media and WIG-clothes are the indices which were most negatively impacted by COVID-19 on the event day. The WIG-pharmaceuticals index experienced negative and statistically significant abnormal rates of returns on the second day prior to the event day, on the event day and one day after. Over the days following the event, the sector index exhibited impressive positive abnormal returns, however, the cumulative average abnormal rate of return for the 11-day window is not statistically significant (see table 3). The two other indices revealed a negative performance almost every day following the event. These results show that investors expected that the possible implementation of a lockdown policy meant poor prospects for companies from WIG-clothes and WIG-media (mainly due to the lower potential advertising revenue expectations caused by the reduced clients' marketing budgets). The reason for this negative performance may be due to the fact that companies from WIG-clothes and also WIG-media had to shut down their businesses.

WIG-telecom and WIG-mining are the indices which were the less sensitive to the shock information with the largest positive statistically significant AR on the event day (these findings are in line with Mazur et al. 2021). However, the results show a negative statistically significant result on the day prior to the WHO announcement (-2.55 %).

After the WHO announcement, almost every sector index shows a significant stock market reaction, except WIG-games, which did not show any significant AR within the event window. This finding implies that WIG-games index was not affected by the WHO announcement in the short-term, however it may be impacted in the long-term.

Table 2. ARs – the FED announcement (April 9, 2020)

Event period day	AR	t-ratio	AR	t-ratio	AR	t-ratio
	WIG-banking		WIG-construction		WIG-chemical	
-5	-2.04	2.7757***	1.04	1.0238	-1.64	1.0502
-4	-2.13	2.8973***	3.17	3.1303***	0.05	0.0299
-3	0.21	0.2897	0.01	0.0028	2.14	1.3720
-2	2.87	3.9114***	-2.93	2.8862***	4.18	2.6742***
-1	-5.34	7.2761***	1.56	1.5396	1.78	1.1395
0	-0.46	0.6288	1.19	1.1736	3.07	1.9643*
+1	-1.16	1.5805	1.93	1.9073*	4.60	2.9420***
+2	-0.62	0.8495	-0.25	0.2448	0.05	0.0310
+3	-0.66	0.8974	0.55	0.5377	2.01	1.2872
+4	-2.17	2.9408***	-0.71	0.7030	-0.90	0.5787
+5	-0.88	1.1940	1.26	1.2460	-2.71	1.7324*

Event period day	AR	t-ratio	AR	t-ratio	AR	t-ratio
	WIG-energy		WIG-games		WIG-mining	
-5	2.50	1.5942	0.34	0.2016	0.01	0.0085
-4	-0.39	0.2464	0.26	0.1557	-0.63	0.4476
-3	0.27	0.1740	1.88	1.1252	2.43	1.7401*
-2	-0.70	0.4484	-7.62	4.5634***	3.50	2.5034**
-1	-1.10	0.7051	3.23	1.9322*	-0.04	0.0279
0	**-1.09**	**0.6965**	**0.57**	**0.3394**	**-0.44**	**0.3116**
+1	-1.08	0.6886	-0.31	0.1834	3.07	2.1953**
+2	2.33	1.4885	2.34	1.3983	-1.59	1.1360
+3	5.11	3.2666***	-0.12	0.0716	0.58	0.4177
+4	-0.65	0.4118	1.30	0.7806	0.20	0.1453
+5	-0.86	0.5486	2.96	1.7708*	-0.28	0.1981
	WIG-IT		WIG-pharmaceuticals		WIG-media	
-5	-0.32	0.3146	3.56	1.4862	-0.86	0.5508
-4	-1.49	1.4529	15.64	6.5356***	-0.92	0.5909
-3	1.29	1.2528	4.92	2.0545**	-1.24	0.7938
-2	-2.03	1.9735**	-10.71	4.4746***	2.04	1.3029
-1	1.99	1.9408*	-1.88	0.7834	1.17	0.7477
0	**-0.41**	**0.4022**	**-3.81**	**1.5915**	**5.82**	**3.7289***
+1	2.64	2.5665**	-7.63	3.1890***	3.51	2.2485**
+2	0.02	0.0195	2.55	1.0646	-0.72	0.4627
+3	0.19	0.1863	2.26	0.9432	-0.97	0.6181
+4	0.27	0.2590	-0.65	0.2707	3.06	1.9619*
+5	-1.57	1.5278	-0.62	0.2579	2.33	1.4917
	WIG-automobiles&parts		WIG-real estate		WIG-clothes	
-5	0.20	0.1624	-0.93	1.0322	-4.29	3.1255***
-4	0.27	0.2263	-0.58	0.6488	0.27	0.2004
-3	2.97	2.4726**	-2.02	2.2393**	2.66	1.9405*
-2	-3.50	2.9130***	3.00	3.3254***	2.95	2.1491**
-1	-0.36	0.2969	2.71	3.0082***	2.11	1.5418
0	**1.81**	**1.5067**	**-0.24**	**0.2658**	**1.17**	**0.8542**
+1	10.89	9.0732***	2.07	2.2949**	1.72	1.2520
+2	-1.76	1.4656	-2.31	2.5645***	2.39	1.7412*
+3	2.10	1.7487*	1.99	2.2065**	-3.11	2.2669**
+4	1.46	1.2155	2.14	2.3787**	1.98	1.4442
+5	1.54	1.2840	-0.75	0.8361	-0.02	0.0134

Event period day	AR	t-ratio	AR	t-ratio	AR	t-ratio
	WIG-oil&gas		WIG-food		WIG-telecom	
-5	6.10	4.2047***	-0.60	0.4615	0.29	0.1928
-4	1.71	1.1782	-0.55	0.4220	1.20	0.7914
-3	0.44	0.2998	3.73	2.8873***	-3.36	2.2150**
-2	-0.29	0.1991	-0.35	0.2697	-1.49	0.9823
-1	1.35	0.9318	0.72	0.5604	7.43	4.8941***
0	**-1.73**	**1.1920**	**0.52**	**0.4011**	**1.90**	**1.2545**
+1	-2.52	1.7381*	1.70	1.3188	-4.27	2.8150***
+2	-0.55	0.3794	-0.44	0.3419	0.16	0.1073
+3	-0.90	0.6220	3.25	2.5187**	-2.00	1.3158
+4	0.11	0.0775	-0.37	0.2859	0.57	0.3733
+5	0.03	0.0199	-0.13	0.1001	2.27	1.4934

***, **, * significant at 1 %, 5 %, 10 % respectively
Source: author's own elaboration.

The findings (see Table 2) confirm that the stimulus package announced by the FED created positive statistically significant abnormal returns for only two industry indices: WIG-chemicals (AR=3.07 %) and WIG-media (AR=5.82 %). Due to the results, the FED announcement did not create negative statistically significant abnormal returns on the event day for any industry index, however, it did it on the day prior to the FED declaration for WIG-banking index. The explanation of this result may be in the fact that investors predicted such an announcement and reacted before the official date of the event.

After the FED announcement, every sector index shows a significant stock market reaction, either on the following day or on further days within the event window. However, in the case of the FED announcement, less abnormal rates of returns can be observed which are statistically significant than in the case of the WHO announcement. This could suggest that the WSE investors were less sensitive to the FED stimulus package announcement than to the WHO declaration regarding the COVID-19 pandemic outbreak.

In the cases of seven WIG indices the positive abnormal returns, which are statistically significant, can be observed on the days following the event (delayed response).

Table 3 presents parametric tests results for the cumulative average abnormal returns around the first event for the 11 and 21-day window.

Table 3. CARs – the WHO announcement (March 11, 2020)

	Market model			
	CAR (-5,+5)	t-ratio	CAR (10,+10)	t-ratio
WIG-banking	-10.07	5.4059***	-6.75	2.7556***
WIG-construction	-8.32	2.7056***	-5.01	1.2158
WIG-chemical	11.61	2.4463**	14.91	2.2541**
WIG-energy	10.37	2.1369**	8.80	1.2943
WIG-games	6.66	1.3241	11.16	1.6475
WIG-mining	11.60	2.6132***	17.23	2.8031***
WIG-IT	-0.23	0.0704	-0.56	0.1286
WIG-pharmaceuticals	-3.23	0.5200	-14.09	1.6251
WIG-media	-21.00	5.5049***	-24.41	4.8703***
WIG-automobiles&parts	-19.09	5.6094***	-31.07	7.5692***
WIG-real estate	-9.34	4.1046***	-19.51	6.3026***
WIG-clothes	-18.67	4.7293***	-10.50	1.9336*
WIG-oil&gas	9.44	2.4922**	12.58	2.4493**
WIG-food	-9.19	3.0760***	-11.75	2.9336***
WIG-telecom	13.31	2.9722***	1.99	0.3213

***, **, * significant at 1 %, 5 %, 10 % respectively
Source: author's own elaboration.

As seen in table 3, seven out of fifteen indices exhibit negative and statistically significant cumulative average abnormal rates of return (WIG-media, WIG-automobiles&parts, WIG-clothes, WIG-real estate, WIG-banking, WIG-food, WIG-construction). The lowest value of CAR was exhibited by WIG-media (CAR= -21 %) and WIG-automobiles&parts (CAR= -19.09 %), WIG-clothes (CAR= -18.67 %), WIG-banking (CAR= -10.07 %). These indices performed worse on CAR compared to others due the fact that COVID-19 reduced the demand for the products and services operated by companies from these industries (mainly due to the lockdown policy, travel restrictions, possible wage cuts, interest rates cuts).

Five indices exhibit positive and statistically significant cumulative average abnormal rates of return (WIG-chemicals, WIG-energy, WIG-mining, WIG-oil&gas, WIG-telecom). The highest value of CAR was exhibited by WIG-telecom (13.31 %) and WIG-chemicals (11.61 %). The companies from WIG-telecom performed better on CAR compared to others due the fact that COVID-19 enhanced the demand for the products and services supporting work from home. Additionally, companies from WIG-chemicals do relatively well, as the demand for chemical products increased due to the pandemic.

These results are in line with prior studies conducted by (i.a. Chen/Chen/Tang/Huang (2009), Alam et al. (2020) and Ramelli and Wagner (2020).

The other indices (WIG-IT, WIG-pharmaceuticals and WIG-games) show no clear evidence of being affected by the WHO announcement in the short-term. (In the case of the other indices the cumulative average abnormal rates of return are not statistically significant).

Figure 1 and figure 2 illustrate how the values of the CARs changed over time within the 11-day window around the first (March 11, 2020) and the second event (April 9, 2020).

Figure 1. CARs within the period (-5;5) – the WHO announcement (March 11, 2020)

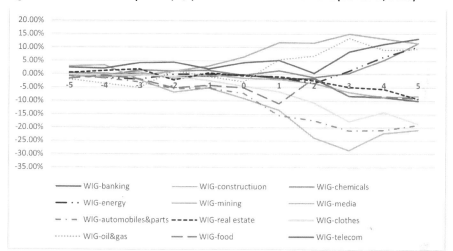

* The figure presents only statistically significant results.
Source: author's own elaboration.

The results presented in Figure 1 support the conclusions that COVID-19 has had a heterogenous effect on sector indices of the WSE. It is seen that the sector indices formulated three groups – the group which perform well in the crisis (WIG-telecom, WIG-mining, WIG-oil&gas, WIG-energy and WIG-chemicals), the group which was less resistant to COVID-19 (WIG-real estate, WIG-construction, WIG-food, WIG-banking) and the group which was the most negatively vulnerable to the COVID-19 outbreak (WIG-clothes, WIG-automobiles&parts, WIG-media).

Table 4. CARs – the FED announcement (April 9, 2020)

	Market model			
	CAR (-5,+5)	(t-ratio)	CAR (-10,+10)	(t-ratio)
WIG-banking	-12.35	(5.0771)***	-23.00	(6.9381)***
WIG-construction	6.82	(2.0283)**	14.38	(3.1426)***
WIG-chemicals	12.63	(2.4358)**	20.31	(2.8232)***
WIG-energy	4.35	(0.8376)	1.06	(0.1465)
WIG-games	4.82	(0.8700)	9.69	(1.2720)
WIG-mining	6.84	(1.4741)	4.97	(0.7746)
WIG-IT	0.57	(0.1670)	6.15	(1.3067)
WIG-pharmaceuticals	3.63	(0.4574)	4.10	(0.3755)
WIG-media	13.22	(2.5524)**	0.01	(0.0009)
WIG-automobiles&parts	15.62	(3.9239)***	22.06	(4.1785)***
WIG-real estate	5.07	(1.6966)*	3.45	(0.8336)
WIG-clothes	7.84	(1.7239)*	6.50	(1.0311)
WIG-oil&gas	3.74	(0.7783)	10.30	(1.5701)
WIG-food	7.50	(1.7504)*	8.64	(1.5269)
WIG-telecom	2.70	(0.5363)	-0.51	(0.0727)

***, **, * significant at 1 %, 5 %, 10 % respectively
Source: author's own elaboration.

As seen in Table 4, only one index – WIG-banking exhibited negative and statistically significant cumulative abnormal returns in the 11-day window (-12.35 %) as well as the 21-day window (-23.00 %). It can be explained by the fact that the Polish banking sector faced difficulties not only due to interest rates cuts, but also due to unresolved issues of the CHF mortgage loans and the tax on assets of certain financial institutions that was introduced in 2016.

The study's results show that only in the case of seven sector indices (WIG-construction, WIG-chemicals, WIG-media, WIG- automobiles&parts, WIG-real estate, WIG-clothes, WIG-food) the results of the CARs are positive and statistically significant in the 11-day window (in the 21-day window the results are statistically significant only for three sector indices).

The CAR analysis confirms the AR findings and suggests that the WSE investors were less sensitive to the FED stimulus package announcement than to the WHO declaration regarding the COVID-19 pandemic outbreak. The still unknown scale and the length of the pandemic could be the most probable explanation. This uncertainty makes the pandemic an unprecedented event and even the declaration regarding the stimulus package announced by the FED is still slightly far from the perfect remedy.

Figure 2. CARs within the period (-5;5) – the FED announcement (April 9, 2020)

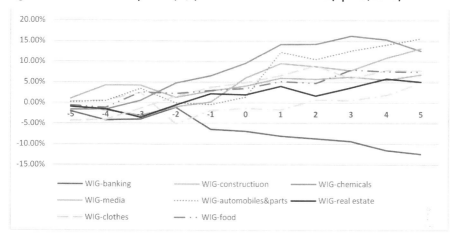

* The figure presents only statistically significant results.
Source: author's own elaboration.

The analysis of the data presented in Figure 2 also supports the conclusions that COVID-19 has had a heterogenous effect on sector indices of the WSE. However, in the case of the FED announcement, lower vulnerability of the sector indices to the event can be observed. The sector indices also formulated three groups – two groups which perform (differently) well and one group (only the WIG-banking index) that revealed a negative CAR value. WIG-automobiles&parts, WIG-media and WIG-chemicals were the indices which revealed the highest values of CARs within the short 11-day window. The first two indices were the indices which were negatively affected by the WHO announcement.

It should be taken into account that at the beginning of 2020 the Polish banking system was well prepared for the crisis in terms of the capital level and liquidity, in December 2019 Tier 1 was equal to 17 %. The problem of the Polish banking sector was the deteriorating operational efficiency. Before the COVID-19 pandemic outbreak, the high level of fiscal burdens on the banking sector caused a significant reduction in operational efficiency indicators. The pandemic has aggravated the negative trends. The average return on equity (ROE) of the banking sector decreased from 6.7 % in December 2019 to 3.7 % in September 2020, and the return on assets (ROA) fell from 0.7 % to 0.4 %. The FED's decision in the field of the monetary policy could indicate similar actions undertaken by the Polish central bank. The Monetary Policy Council made significant cuts in the level of interest rates (the reference rate was decreased to the lowest level – 0.1 % so far). The reason for the negative reaction of the WIG-banking index to the FED's statement may be due to the investors' concerns regarding the level of interest margins. Later months of 2020 confirmed that these concerns were justified. The net profit of the banking sector in Poland in September 2020 was 49.2 % lower than in the corresponding period of 2019, and the main reason was the erosion of deposit margins and the lower scale of operations (Polish Financial Supervision Authority, https://www.knf.gov.pl/en/).

Conclusions

The COVID-19 outbreak affected not only people's health and social life, but also companies and the financial markets all around the world. The consequences of COVID-19 are uncertain and diverse. As Ellul/Erel/Rajan (2020) claim: "corporations, whether small, medium, or large, young or old, are at the very heart of these two challenges, and academic research will be needed to guide policy making".

This study uses event study methodology to examine the COVID-19 impact on the stock market indices of the Warsaw Stock Exchange – the largest stock exchange in Central and Eastern Europe. The results show how investors' confidence has changed since the official WHO announcement of the pandemic outbreak, but there is a great variation among the indices.

The general findings indicate that COVID-19 had a heterogenous effect on sector indices of the WSE. The study results confirm that on the Polish stock market the quotations of WIG-clothes, WIG-automobiles&parts, WIG-media were most negatively vulnerable to the COVID-19 outbreak. This negative reaction may be due to the lockdown and travel restrictions which caused many companies from these indexes to stop doing business. COVID-19 negatively affected the demand not only for clothes and cars, but also for marketing services. Investors were very sensitive to the pandemic news and expected that a possible quarantine policy would cause bad prospects for these sectors. A negative performance of the media/ communication sector was observed on the Australian market (Narayan et al., 2021).

WIG-telecom, WIG-mining, WIG-oil&gas, WIG-energy and WIG-chemicals performed well in the pandemic. The results for the telecom sector are in line with prior research conducted on the US market (Ramelli and Wagner (2020), Mazur et al. (2021) and on the Australian market (Alam et al. (2020), Narayan et al. (2021)). This positive reaction could be explained by the increasing demand for distance work and learning caused by the lockdown policy implemented by the governments, which was country independent. Similarly, the positive results for the chemicals sector could be explained by the enhanced demand for the products offered by companies from the sector (especially against viruses), therefore, the investors expected good future prospects.

The study's results for mining are in line with Mazur et al. (2021), however, the findings for energy, oil & gas sectors are not consistent with the prior research (Alam et al. (2020), Ramelli and Wagner (2020), Narayan et al. (2021). The sectors, all over the world, which consist of upstream oil and gas production suffered strongly due to the oil price decline in March 2020, caused by the oil price between Saudi Arabia and Russia. Polish companies can be classified as downstream oil and gas production companies, therefore, the drop in the oil and gas prices allows achieving a higher margin. On the other hand, there was a negative factor – the concerns regarding the rapidly shrinking demand for petrochemical products, caused by the lockdowns. Therefore, the positive reaction of the WIG-oil&gas could mean that the investors' expectations of higher margins prevailed over the concerns regarding the decreasing demand.

The real estate index was less resistant to COVID-19, which is consistent with the findings of Alam (2020) for the Australian market and Mazur et al. (2020) for the US market. As on other markets, COVID-19 caused an economic slowdown in Poland, as a consequence the demand for the real estate industry decreased (people were afraid of losing jobs or possible wage cuts).

The study results revealed mostly a positive reaction of sector indices reaction to the FED announcement regarding the stimulus action. However, in the case of this event, less statistically significant results can be observed than in the case of the WHO announcement. This could suggest that the WSE investors were less sensitive to the FED stimulus package announcement than to the WHO declaration regarding the COVID-19 pandemic outbreak.

The negative reaction of the WIG-banking to the FED announcement could be surprising, however, it may be due to the situation in the Polish banking sector, which was characterised by the high level of fiscal burdens, which caused a significant reduction in the operational efficiency indicators. The pandemic aggravated the negative trends. As a consequence, a negative WIG-banking reaction could be observed, which indicates the investors' concerns regarding the level of the interest margins and the profitability of the banking sector in the future.

The research results suggest that the political and legal environment may have a significant impact on the reaction of stock indices to shocking situations such as the COVID-19 pandemic. Another issue, important for the reaction, is the fact that on less developed capital markets, the limited number of listed companies may mean that the sector index is not very well diversified (or otherwise, highly concentrated), therefore, it strongly depends on one or two companies with the highest capitalisation. A change in the price of this main company may then strongly affect the sector index. This problem does not occur in large capital markets. This could be the reason for the differences in the study results between Poland and more developed capital markets.

To the best of the authors' knowledge, this research is the first attempt to analyse the COVID-19 implications on the sector indices on the WSE. With the results of this study the investors and company managers will have a better idea about which sectors are risky in the case of the COVID-19 pandemic in order to take precautions accordingly. The results could be also interesting for the government institutions which should offer assistance and support.

This study is based on the short-term reaction on the COVID-19 events, therefore, further research could examine the long-term impacts of COVID-19 on different sector indices of the stock exchange.

Acknowledgments:

The authors thank the Guest Editor, Thomas Steger and the two anonymous reviewers for their constructive comments, recommendations and support.

Reference list

Akhtaruzzaman, M./Boubaker, S./Sensoy, A. (2020): Financial contagion during COVID-19 crisis, in: Finance Research Letters, doi:10.1016/j.frl.2020.101604.

Alam, M.M./Wei, H./Wahid, A.N.M. (2020): COVID-19 outbreak and sectoral performance of the Australian stock market: An event study analysis. Australian Economic Papers, doi: 10.1111/1467–8454.12215.

Al-Awadhi, A.M./Alsaifi, K./Al-Awadhi, A./Alhammadi, S. (2020): Death and contagious infectious diseases: Impact of the COVID-19 virus on stock market returns, in: Journal of Behavioral and Experimental Finance, doi: 10.1016/j.jbef.2020.100326.

Ali, M./Alam, N./Rizvi, S.A.R. (2020): Coronavirus (COVID-19)–An epidemic or pandemic for financial markets, in: Journal of Behavioral and Experimental Finance, vol. 27, 100341. https://doi.org/10.1016/j.jbef.2020.100341.

Ashraf, B. N. (2020): Stock markets' reaction to COVID-19: cases or fatalities?, in: Research in International Business and Finance, doi:10.1016/j.ribaf.2020.101249.

Baker, S. R./Bloom, N./Davis, S. J./Kost, K./Sammon, M./Viratyosin, T. (2020): The unprecedented stock market reaction to COVID-19, in: The Review of Asset Pricing Studies, doi:10.1093/rapstu/raaa008.

Brown, S. J./Warner, J. B. (1980): Measuring security price performance. Journal of financial economics, 8(3), 205–258.

Brown, S.J./Warner, J.B. (1985): Using Daily Stock Returns. The case of Event Studies, in: Journal of Financial Economics, 14, 3–31.

BSE (2021): available at: https://www.bse.hu/pages/cash-market#equities (18/05/2021).

BSSE (2021): available at: http://www.bsse.sk/bcpben/SecuritiesMarkets/Securities/tabid/303/language/en-US/Default.aspx?Market=H (18/05/2021).

Cao, K.H./Li, Q./Liu, Y./Woo, C.K. (2020): Covid-19's adverse effects on a stock market index, in: Applied Economics Letters, 1–5, doi: 13504851.2020.1803481.

Chen, C. D./Chen, C. C./Tang, W. W./Huang, B. Y. (2009): The positive and negative impacts of the SARS outbreak: A case of the Taiwan industries, in: The Journal of Developing Areas, 281–293.

Chen, H.C./Yeh, C.W. (2021): Global financial crisis and COVID-19: Industrial reactions. Finance Research Letters, doi: 10.1016/j.frl.2021.101940.

Czech, K./Wielechowski, M./Kotyza, P./Benešová, I./Laputková, A. (2020): Shaking Stability: COVID-19 Impact on the Visegrad Group Countries' Financial Markets, in: Sustainability, 12, 15, 6282.

Ding, W./Levine, R.E./Lin, C./Xie, W. (2020): Corporate Immunity to the COVID-19 Pandemic, in: Journal of Financial Economics, doi: 10.2139/ssrn.3578585.

Ellul, A./Erel, I./ Rajan, U. (2020): The COVID-19 Pandemic Crisis and Corporate Finance, in: The Review of Corporate Finance Studies, 9, 3, 421–429, doi: 10.1093/rcfs/cfaa016.

Espinoza-Mendez, C./Arias, J. (2020): COVID-19 effect on herding behaviour in European Capital Markets, in: Finance Research Letters, doi:10.1016/j.frl.2020.101787.

Harjoto, M. A./Rossi, F./Lee, R./Kownatzki, C. (2020 a): COVID-19: Risk-adjusted portfolio returns of emerging and developed equity markets, in: Journal of Risk Management in Financial Institutions, 14, 1, 72–83.

Harjoto, M. A./Rossi, F./Paglia, J. K. (2020 b): COVID-19: Stock market reactions to the shock and the stimulus, in: Applied Economics Letters, 10 1–7, doi: 10.1080/13504851.2020.1781767.

He, P./Sun, Y./Zhang, Y./Li, T. (2020): COVID-19's impact on stock prices across different sectors—An event study based on the Chinese stock market, in: Emerging Markets Finance and Trade, 56(10), 2198–2212.

Heyden, K.J./Heyden, T. (2021): Market reactions to the arrival and containment of COVID-19: an event study, in: Finance research letters, 38, doi: 10.1016/j.frl.2020.101745.

KNF (2021): available at: https://www.knf.gov.pl/en/ (27/09/2021).

Liu, H./Manzoor, A./Wang, C./Zhang, L./Manzoor, Z. (2020): The COVID-19 outbreak and affected countries stock markets response, in: International Journal of Environmental Research and Public Health, 17, 8, doi: 10.3390/ijerph17082800.

Mazur, M./ Dang, M./ Vega, M. (2021): COVID-19 and the march 2020 stock market crash. Evidence from S&P1500, in: Finance Research Letters, doi:10.1016/j.frl.2020.101690.

Narayan, P. K./Devpura, N./Hua, W. (2020): Japanese currency and stock market—What happened during the COVID-19 pandemic?, in: Economic Analysis and Policy, doi:10.1016/j.eap.2020.09.014.

Narayan, P. K./Phan, D. H. B./Liu, G. (2021): COVID-19 lockdowns, stimulus packages, travel bans, and stock returns, in: Finance research letters, 38, doi:10.1016/j.frl.2020.101732.

Narayan, P.K./Gong, Q./Ali Ahmed, H.J. (2021): Is there a pattern in how COVID-19 has affected Australia's stock returns?, in: Applied Economics Letters, doi: 10.1080/13504851.2020.1861190.

Phan, D.H.B./Narayan, P.K. (2020): Country responses and the reaction of the stock market to COVID-19—A preliminary exposition, in: Emerging Markets Finance and Trade, 56 (10), 2138–2150, doi:10.1080/1540496X.2020.1784719.

PSE (2021): available at: https://www.pse.cz/en/market-data (18/05/2021).

Rahman, M.L./Amin, A. S./Al Mamun, M.A. (2021): The COVID-19 Outbreak and Stock Market Reactions: Evidence from Australia, in: Finance Research Letters, doi: 10.2139/ssrn.3773839.

Ramelli, S./Wagner A.F. (2020): Feverish Stock Price Reactions to COVID-19, in: Swiss Finance Institute Research Paper No. 20–12.

Roubini, N. (2020): Coronavirus pandemic has delivered the fastest, deepest economic shock in history, in: The guardian, 25(March).

Topcu, M./Gulal, O.S. (2020): The impact of COVID-19 on emerging stock markets, in: Finance Research Letters, 36, doi:10.1016/j.frl.2020.101691.

World Economic Forum-WEF (2020) How China can rebuild global supply chain resilience after COVID- 19. https://www.weforum.org/agenda/2020/03/coronavirus-and-global-supply-chains/.

Xiong, H./Wu, Z./Hou, F./Zhang, J. (2020): Which firm-specific characteristics affect the market reaction of Chinese listed companies to the COVID-19 pandemic?, in: Emerging Markets Finance and Trade, 56(10), 2231–2242.

Yan, C. (2020): COVID-19 Outbreak and stock prices: Evidence from China. doi: 10.2139/ssrn.3574374.

Zhang, D./Hu, M./Ji, Q. (2020): Financial markets under the global pandemic of COVID-19, in: Finance Research Letters, 36, doi:10.1016/j.frl.2020.101528.

Taming discontinuity: evolution of managerial perceptions, emotions and actions in the pandemic environment. Evidence from Poland*

Krzysztof Obłój, Mariola Ciszewska-Mlinarič, Aleksandra Wąsowska, Piotr Wójcik, Tadeusz Milancej**

Abstract

In this research note we address a question as to how discontinuity caused by the COVID-19 outbreak impacts upon management. The study findings reveal that: (i) the most important impact of the pandemic on management is the introduction of remote working and digitalization of many organizational activities; (ii) the combination of the pandemic situation and remote working produces an impetus for mostly-incremental adaptations in the areas of human resource management, marketing & sales and operations; (iii) the pattern of adaptive responses to the discontinuity is regulated by combinations of evolving managerial perceptions and emotions; (iv) the pandemic confronts managers with new questions and challenges, allowing them to receive important personal 'lessons'.

Keywords: pandemic environment, organizational adaptation, managerial perception, managerial emotions.
JEL Codes: L25, M10, M19

Introduction

The study of organizations is essentially research into environmental and organizational change, and an extensive body of knowledge on the topic has by now been accumulated. This led to many classifications of environmental disturbances and typologies of organizational change (Van de Ven/Poole 1995; Tsoukas/Chia 2002; Micelotta/Lounsbury/Greenwood 2017; Cameron/Green 2020), but none of these prepared managers to face the event that was the

---

* Received: 11.8.20, Accepted: 4.1.21, 2 revisions
** *Krzysztof Obłój*, PhD, Prof. (Corresponding Author), Department of Strategy, Kozminski University and University of Warsaw, Warsaw, Poland. Email: kobloj@kozminski.edu.pl. Main research interests: strategy, international business, entrepreneurship.
Mariola Ciszewska-Mlinarič, PhD, Assoc. Prof., Department of Strategy, Kozminski University, Warsaw, Poland. Email: mariolac@kozminski.edu.pl. Main research interests: internationalization strategy of emerging market firms, internationalisation process and decision-making, and relational capabilities.
Aleksandra Wąsowska, PhD, Assoc. Prof., Faculty of Management, University of Warsaw, Warsaw, Poland. Email: awasowska@wz.uw.edu.pl. Main research interests: strategies of emerging markets' multinationals.
Piotr Wójcik, PhD, Assist. Prof., Department of Strategy, Kozminski University. Email: pwojcik@kozminski.edu.pl. Main research interests: strategy, dynamic capabilities, international business.
Tadeusz Milancej, MA, Assist. Prof., Department of Strategy, Kozminski University. Email: tmilancej@kozminski.edu.pl., Main research interests: behavioral strategy, corporate governance.

pandemic arising in 2020. Our paper therefore addresses the simple but timely question: *how does such an unprecedented situation impact upon management in business organizations?* We do not frame our question as a particular research gap or formulate any hypotheses, because existing theories of adaptation and change do not address situations failing to arise repeatedly. Instead, our aim is to identify, through empirical research and critical thinking, the rhythm and domains of change in organizations facing the unique pandemic environment. Specifically we focus on the nature of the disruptions that firms faced, the ways these changed over time and the ways companies addressed them and why, the actions proving to be most effective, and the emotions the pandemic triggered in companies studied and ways in which these evolved over time.

We are partially guided in our research by the existing body of knowledge on organizational reactions to environmental dynamism (Teece/Pisano/Shuen 1997; Obloj/Obloj/Pratt, 2010), environmental jolts or disruptions (Tushman/Anderson 1986; Meyer/Brooks/Goes 1990; Christensen 2013), the unique situations provided by massive economic shocks (like the global crisis of 2007 and onwards), political transformations like the political and economic systemic change ongoing in the CEECs (Ciszewska-Mlinarič/Obloj/Wasowska 2018), and wars (see Virtual Special Issue of SMJ, April 2020).

Our research note is structured as follows. We first propose a brief statement of our research methods. In following sections we detail research results based upon three subsequent waves of questionnaires sent to the same group of managers. We then conclude with a discussion on the implications and limitations of our findings.

Methods

We adopted a longitudinal approach with three returning waves of e-mail surveying with open-ended questions, separated by the same amount of time (one month). Each time we used the same set of questions plus new supplementary ones reflecting the emerging challenges. We developed a draft questionnaire consisting of 13 open-ended questions covering: (1) the disruptions created by the pandemic as arranged in terms of importance, (2) managers' reactions and the justifications for them, and (3) ways of coping. We then interviewed top managers of comparable firms – not belonging to our sample – to validate our approach. These interviews led to several revisions in our questionnaire, whose final form (see Appendix 1) consisted of open questions supplemented by questions regarding the rationale behind decisions and particular actions.

Faced with time pressure and a limited willingness of Polish managers to respond to questionnaires, we decided to use a convenience database of approximately 800 Executive MBA Polish students at Kozminski University, most of them members of Executive Boards of different companies operating in Poland.

We started our research when the first lockdown was announced in Poland, and emailing the first survey on 5th April (wave 1). By sending a follow-up message we received 110 questionnaires (i.e. a response rate of approximately 14 %).

We repeated our survey one month later, on 4th May (wave 2). We added three questions to our questionnaire (triggered by managerial responses received during wave 1 and pandemic measures introduced by the Polish government), as related to matters of relationships with major stakeholders, emotions and attitudes in firms during lockdowns, and personal feelings and stress levels of respondents. On this occasion, 85 questionnaires from within the initial group of 110 were received back in the wake of the follow-up message.

In the third wave we emailed the slightly-extended questionnaire on 5th June. Following managerial responses of the second wave, we added questions relating to the scope of online communication and work in respondents' firms, and evaluations of support programs put into effect by the Polish state administration. After the follow-up message, 70 questionnaires were returned from within the initial group of 110. All surveys were in Polish and answered via e-mail. Respondents could use as much space as they wanted to answer the questions. Our research waves coincided with main governmental measures employed (i.e. lockdown, four economic refreezing stages and three governmental 'Shields' – i.e. support programs for companies (see Figure 1). We were therefore not only able to address issues of business responses to environmental jolts, and study them in real-time, but also to take into account measures employed by the Polish government – together with the related reactions and emotions of managers.

Our sample is not representative of a Polish economy dominated by incorporated persons, micro, small and medium-sized firms. Rather, it is skewed toward larger firms (as measured by numbers of employees and turnover), location (Warsaw is overrepresented), internationalization (a significant percentage of firms exporting), and online presence. In our sample, 41 % firms have at least 250 employees, 45 % are firms with revenues in 2019 above 100 M PLN (app. 23.5M EUR), and 60 % are firms with an international focus (exporters). While we acknowledge the limitations of our non-representative sample, we follow previous studies (e.g. Shelton/Hein/Phipps 2019) in arguing that a convenience sample of MBA alumni offers a reasonable approximation of behaviors of professional managers. We believe that this sample is 'good enough' for emerging patterns of reactions to the pandemic situation among corporate decision-makers to be observed. Moreover, because our findings correspond with the key message behind several surveys of similar scope that were carried out by well-known institutions at that time in Poland (e.g. PwC, 2020; CMSG 2020), our study is a good approximation of the actual reaction of the entire population of firms in the studied period.

While collecting the raw data from our respondents (i.e. their written answers), we created a database identifying particular responses to each question in each phase of the study. To analyze the data, we employed a combination of grounded theory and temporal bracketing complementary approaches (Gehman/Glaser/Eisenhardt/Gioia/Langley/Corley 2017). We first used a narrative sensemaking strategy to create a story from the raw data and sequenced key events chronologically. We then coded the written answers following the Gioia methodology (Gioia/Corley/Hamilton 2013) to create emergent themes (first-order concepts), which were subsequently refined, and aggregated into second-order categories. Finally, in the iterative process of analyzing emerging categories from the data and re-categorization (Glaser/Strauss 1999), we created final categories including managerial reflections, emotions and organizational actions (see Figure 2 and 3), as presented briefly in the Research findings section below. In some instances, we counted the frequencies of occurrence of quantitative-type responses (whereby respondents could make a selection from a list of options, for instance in regard to particular actions taken).

Figure 1. Timeline of research stages and government actions

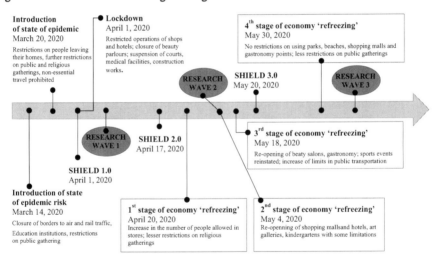

Source: own research

Research findings

First stage: pandemic as a business challenge

Managers reported that the pandemic created a multitude of general and specific disruptions in February and March. Those mentioned most frequently were the need to switch to online communication, restrictions imposed on travel and business meetings, and growing employee concerns. Apart from these common disturbances, managers indicated an almost infinite number of disruptions specific to the industry or their business situation – from falling demand for insurance or mortgage loans, cessation of the process by which permits are granted by the state or local administration, disruptions of operations of courts and notaries, difficulties with the production of advertisements, transportation stoppages, resignation of recipients from providing services at their offices or plants, volatile exchange-rate changes, absences of employees, lack of hygiene and healthcare materials, legislative chaos and general uncertainty. The most important and systemic disruptions were created by lockdown regulations (see Appendix 1), which closed selected markets and distribution channels, limited general mobility, and forced firms to adopt an online mode of operation. Kindergartens and school closures also excluded some employees from company operations. As a result, demand fell and supply chains were broken. Our findings resonate with the study which showed that 2/3 of surveyed SMEs limited their activities in the aftermath of pandemic, and reported problems resulting mostly from decrease in demand, delays in payments from customers and supply chain disruptions. For more than one third of the surveyed companies, the decrease in revenues exceeded 50 % compared to the same period last year (PwC 2020).

In spite of all these disruptions and general anxiety, managers tried to take control of the situation, adopting solutions to deal with major disturbances one by one. The most common first reactions included: moving wherever possible to remote operations (80 % of indications), limiting visits of suppliers and customers in the company (70 % of indications), implementation of new procedures and measures in occupational hygiene and safety (68 % of indications), and cost reduction (over 50 %). Hence, at this stage (April 2020) managers perceived the pandemic as a human-resources and operational-management challenge, not as a survival threat to their organizations. Respondents claimed to have remained calm and even to have been satisfied with the number of issues they had to deal with. They reported a feeling of control over the situation, and allocated time and attention to key processes and clients, continuity of supplies, strict safety and hygiene-protection procedures, and efforts to reduce costs through renegotiation as regards supply conditions, rents, distribution costs and inventory. Interestingly, the need for a reduction in employment or salaries was rarely indicated.

Most managers also reported putting major emphasis on relations and communication with employees and customers (62 out of 110 collected responses i.e.

56%). Employees were in the foreground, as the head of a large industrial company emphasized: *"I am very happy and at the same time proud of all my employees, who show remarkable maturity, resourcefulness and openness"*. The second most important group were clients – for whom respondents shortened lead times, adjusted offers to individual requirements, and also – as an expression of their understanding for liquidity problems – postponed payments. The scale and speed of disruptions demanded many managerial reactions over a short period of time, and – as one respondent wrote: *"we try to navigate a ship like a racing boat"*. Figure 2 illustrates managerial moves that impacted mainly on the areas of human resources, operations management and (to a lesser degree) marketing.

Figure 2. The impact of the pandemic and administrative lockdown on management (research stage I)

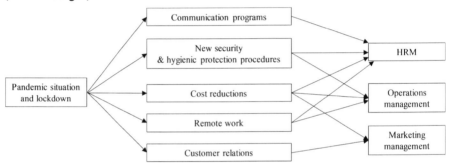

Second stage: adapting to the pandemic

The analysis of answers provided by managers in the second (May 2020) round of research indicated that in spite of the lasting lockdown, nearly 80% of respondents felt they were coping well with pandemic challenges, while another 20% emphasized that they had managed to keep the situation under control. The main driver of this attitude was a perception that employees, customers, suppliers and companies in general had accustomed themselves to the new reality. The introduction of massive state-support programs for individual entrepreneurs, SMEs and large enterprises (entailing tax relief or deferrals, subsidies and loans) also improved both the prospects and climate for business.

Most of the disruptions perceived resembled those of March, as they included: outflows of customers and difficulty in acquiring new ones; supply chain disruptions (limited availability of supplies, delivery delays, price increases); distribution disruptions (store closures, reduced availability of distribution channels); problems in contacting key partners due to mobility restrictions and employee-related problems (sick leaves and care leaves); and a deterioration in customer payment discipline. The new disturbances related mostly to the competitive situation, psychological discomfort and the negative consequences of operations being digitized. On that basis, adaptive adjustments were mostly again triggered in the areas of marketing and sales, HRM and operations.

First, managers began to notice that the "market cake" was shrinking, due to aggressive competitive actions and a deterioration in the business environment. Many companies indicated that the crisis had become a testing ground for relationships with customers and competitors alike, because – as one of the respondents pointed out: " *it's a jungle out there, everyone is fighting for survival"*.

To address such growing competitive pressures, managers focused on maintaining sales revenues through the digitization of marketing activities; an intensive search for new customers; investment in online sales; training of the salesforce in new modes of operation; and application for government grants, subsidies and loans. Acquisition of the latter typically improved companies' financial standing, and allowed them to organize marketing campaigns and develop new distribution channels, especially of the ecommerce-type. The vast majority of respondents declared that they were already planning for the time beyond the pandemic. There was a belief that an influence on reality could be regained: "*We return to normal modes. We are planning sales campaigns. We're going forward"*.

Second, managers reported increasing psychological discomfort in their firms. Employees' moods varied and depended to a large extent on how strong the previous impact of the pandemic had been. In companies experiencing its consequences only mildly, that mood stabilized – tensions abated, employees started to adapt to the "new normal", there was hope and a feeling that "the worst is behind us". However, in other companies, anxiety and fear of layoffs persisted. Some managers noticed an increase in the involvement of employees who were "*worried about the future, trying harder than usual"*. In some companies, the decline in mood was just beginning. "*The pandemic crisis has reached our company… The mood is not bad, but there is some fear about the future."* Managers felt sympathy for these attitudes because they also pointed to their own personal difficulties in dealing with the pandemic, describing their own anxiety, frustration, exhaustion, tension and chronic stress. One respondent admitted: *" I am convinced that the coming years will be a difficult time where we will fight the recession (...) I think my stress level has been at the highest level for years."* The indicated sources of stress were primarily the difficult financial situation of the companies and family life – whose rhythm had been changed markedly by the rules of social isolation.

To address such concerns, managers took actions relating to people management that steadily became more diverse and systemic. While still caring about health and safety, they also started devoting more time to internal communication with employees, organizing video conferences, discussing activities and the external context, progress with work, but also the well-being of employees: "*The most important for me is contact with my team and maintaining a sense of bond, despite isolation. We organized remote meetings, training sessions, even a short virtual beer parties after business hours – we are still a team connected by a common goal.*" Hence, HRM management became more performance- and climate-oriented, while before it had mostly been focused on communication and the implementation of pandemic-related procedures.

Third, in the area of operations, respondents reported the growing discomfort and tiredness arising out of remote working. There was loneliness, but also fatigue with what was *de facto* around-the-clock online communication. Managers of companies employing salespeople accustomed to frequent visits to customers reported considerable frustration with on-line operations among employees of this group. There was a general feeling that: "*Remote work, which used to be the Holy Grail, suddenly turns out not to be so attractive, and everyone dreams of returning to the office. Occasional visits to it become like a holiday.*"

In general, the pandemic and changes in the overall business and administrative environment led managers to introduce many new, mostly incremental adaptations. They were mostly focused on raising employees' levels of competence (to deal better with the demands of remote working), as well as on the organizational climate, financial stability, future-oriented marketing and sales, and better operational management (see Figure 3).

Figure 3. The pandemic's impact on management (research stage II)

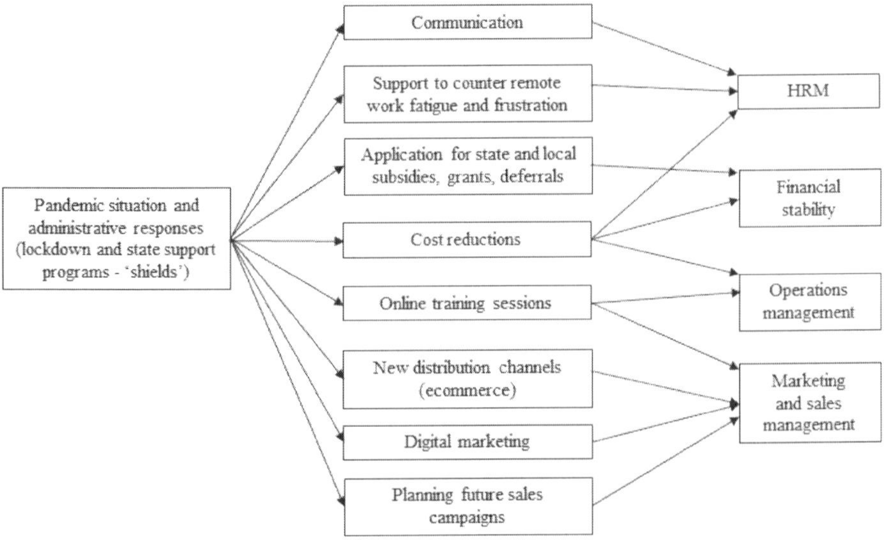

Source: own research

The results of our study confirm the findings of the survey of medium and large companies from that period which reported that nearly 70 % of companies were changing their HR policies and work practices in the wake of the outbreak, and half of the surveyed managers made business plans beyond the pandemic (Navigator Capital Group 2020).

Third stage: caution and growing polarization

The third round of our research (June 2020) coincided with a lifting of most administrative restrictions by the Polish government. Managers were therefore more optimistic.: *"The last four weeks have been a relief, related to the opening-up of the economy."* Approximately 70 % of respondents believed that their companies were doing just as well as in the former period, with another 20 % actually claiming to be doing better, and only 10 % in a worse business situation. Respondents indicated that there were no new disturbances, and that business conditions had improved. Customers were placing new orders, online sales were growing, and supply chains were returning to normal operations. Hence managers started to think about the future: *"Now no matter how bad it is, we don't expect any surprises... We are starting to plan the future, instead of just fighting here and now for survival"*.

However, closer analysis of managerial responses indicated that the plans for the future were mostly short-term and rather incremental. Organizations were focused on the continuation of existing activities and gradual adjustments, rather than on the introduction of new solutions: *"Our actions continue to bring moderate results, but we are slowly moving forward and we understand better the challenges ahead"*. Despite positive assessment of the effectiveness of actions taken hitherto by most of the companies, the respondents underlined the growing uncertainty, and reported that almost all investment projects were being put on hold. Hence, after the short burst of initiatives observable in the second period studied, most companies were adopting 'wait and see' attitude, with managers putting off larger projects, and at best experimenting with change in areas that they found most impactful. The first was related to digital transformation in most companies and the frustration that it brought. With the end of lockdown, companies started to move into hybrid mode, operating partially online and partially on-site. Secondly, some companies were introducing new products and services, including offers from the B2B to B2C segment, or vice versa. Thirdly, many respondents were again preparing for *"hard times ahead"*, reorganizing the workplace and creating crisis teams tasked with monitoring compliance with safety rules and stocks of personal protective equipment, as well as coordinating action where any deterioration in the health situation was arising.

Two management challenges for the future seemed to be developing gradually. First, there was ongoing polarization of relationships with stakeholders. Good relations that had strengthened in the first and second periods remained very stable and supportive, while those that had not been very good before were now deteriorating further. Many managers admitted that the difficult business situation and uncertainty were triggering adverse reactions among different stakeholders. As one manager put it succinctly: *"The first wave of a natural sense of community is giving way to an increasingly fierce competitive struggle"*.

Second, we also observed a growing amplitude to changes in the evaluation of employees' attitudes and moods, from very positive to very pessimistic, in which the future appeared only in terms of uncertainty, fear and weariness. The clear differentiating factor became the business situation. In the companies whose business situation improved (markets rebounded and new orders came), managers observed a lack of clear business threats in the near future and attitudes and moods improved in consequence. The pandemic seemed to have become tamed psychologically, and employees more relaxed and joyful, as companies started to ask selected groups of them to come back to offices (if still following strict hygine regimes). On the other hand, in the firms facing business difficulties, respondents indicated that employees' morale was low, with uncertainty and fear dominating. Former mobilization had given way to conflicts and a fight for survival: *"... the first two months of increased mobilization seem to have passed, and some general resentment started"*.

While these attitudes were influenced by the business situation of particular companies, a further key reason was a growing tiredness with online operations. There had therefore been a clear lifecycle to remote working made manifest in the three waves of our research. The first stage, immediately after the pandemic began, was dominated by positive emotions. Employees learnt to use *Teams, Zoom, GoogleMeets, Webex* and so on, and were experimenting enthusiastically with functions, applications and new possibilities. A normalization stage then ensued, with remote working used massively and for everything. Private and online business life began to mix: " *The line between work and home has been blurred. This gives some savings and opportunities, but also many challenges in terms of efficiency management"*. Online communication and working was starting to bore and irritate people. People came to work even when there was no need for that, and started to complain, and sometimes argue: "*Although before the pandemic they dreamed of working remotely, some want to return to the office. Next week the employees are organizing (a grassroots initiative) some integration meeting. I have no tools to forbid them to do so.*"

Again, our findings are consistent with what Pracodawcy RP's (major organization of Polish employers') survey results that the companies assess their own situation better than the state of the whole economy, that employees' well-being is on top of boardrooms' agendas and that 90 % of surveyed businesses are concerned about the future turn of events, so they focused on cost control and were unwilling to engage in risky endeavors (CMSG 2020).

Discussion

We have been addressing a research question related to Polish companies' reactions to the unique jolt in the overall business environment that pandemic conditions provided. The novelty, multi-dimensionality and life-threatening character of this development has left established theories all but worthless as beacons generating questions and hypotheses, even if they go on providing an important context for our major findings as regards the scope, type and moderators of management adaptive changes to the pandemic situation.

First, research into organizational adaptation and change generally assumes a continuum of two stylized relationships between the macroenvironment and organizational change. Transformative changes are driven by environmental turbulence, while incremental, evolutionary changes mostly respond to external changes that are minor, frequent and predictable. Our research thus reveals an interesting paradox. The pandemic as a circumstance of major turbulence offers an impetus for both transformative and incremental change in the companies studied. The major transformative change entails the implementation of remote working as enforced by the shutdown of the economy and the rules on social distancing that administrative regulations have been imposing. The impact here is major and systemic because in most studied companies it brought change in marketing, sales and supplier-management (thanks to the new lack of direct contacts), in operations management (with remote communication and work other than in factories, as well as cost-cutting), and in HR practices (in line with strict H&S procedures and communication programs).

We cannot know how sustainable the above transformative change is and will be, and what form it will take in the future. For even as it changed the *modus operandi* and communication in many of the organizations studied, it did not change strategies, structures or major procedures. One possible prosaic reason is that it may just be too early to observe transformative changes in organizations; but we also propose that situations of unusually great uncertainty (in which it is difficult to make sense of change in the business environment) simply limit managerial appetite for transformative change.

In the context of the transformative nature of remote operations, it is a repertoire of incremental moves that dominates. Companies adapt and calibrate products and services, marketing campaigns, distribution channels, operations, etc. to the pandemic situation. Forecasting becomes impossible and managers thus prefer to limit risk, and to focus on adaptive, incremental changes in the main functional area of management.

Interestingly, our findings regarding the nature of organizational reactions to this discontinuity resonate with research on dynamic capabilities (DCs) and threat-rigidity phenomenon. While it has been broadly accepted that a hyper-environment enacts major internal transformation of resources and capabilities, including other dynamic capabilities, research about DCs in the face extreme discontinuity remains scarce. What our study might suggest is that firms facing a critical threat to their survival, although undergoing temporal transformation on the operational level, remain rigid on the strategic level (Schilke 2014). We therefore invite future studies to re-examine the link between environmental turbulence, degree of organizational change and the nature of DC, through consideration of an extreme discontinuities' context, for example entailing major crises or environmental jolts.

Second, our research indicates that the pattern of company adaptive responses to the discontinuity created by the pandemic situation is regulated by combinations of managerial perceptions and emotions. The first stage, observable in managerial responses to the first and partially second waves of questionnaires, is driven by perception of the pandemic as a challenge having to be addressed. Managers' perceptions of the business situation revolve around both general disturbances and those of a firm-specific nature: *"We faced disturbances and stagnation, and at the same time a complete lack of information"*. Managers believe that they should keep control of the situation even if emotional costs are high: *"I am tired of work, stress and uncertainty... I think my stress level has been at the highest level for years, which causes health and sleep problems... I am afraid for the future of the company and employees"*.

Notwithstanding a multitude of disruptions and high level of stress, managers have no problems with choosing right responses and changes, because they are driven by external conditions. Particularities of change depend upon contingencies of their business situations, but typically companies invest in a marketing campaign on social media; improve their webpages; add e-commerce to their distribution channels; retrain the salesforce; cut costs through negotiating lower rents and wages and cheaper services; introduce special safety protocols at production sites and in their offices; communicate with employees, diversify their supplier base; and apply for state-support funds and loans. In essence, managers adapt their organizations to immediate demands of a pandemic environment, by means of a recalibration of HRM practices, operations, finance and marketing, and sales management.

It is in the second stage of this evolution (observable in managerial responses to our second- and third-wave questionnaires) that emotions are coming to take a front seat, and becoming major drivers of managerial responses. The pandemic is no longer perceived as a challenge, but as a major discontinuity that generates huge uncertainty of long-term social and economic consequences.

Just as managers were starting to think about the future, they were required to put all projects on hold, switching to wait-and-see mode. Emotionally, however, the pandemic is tamed, almost like a wild animal would be. The new mantra is: *"we have learnt to live with the virus"*, and that drives responses. There are still elements of anxiety and fear, but health, security and hygiene procedures are in place; remote work dominates; and companies operate, even if somehow in slow-motion. Managerial responses focus on immediate concerns to restore business-as-usual conditions: managing strained relations with stakeholders, improving communication with and the motivation of employees tired of remote operations, and improving the financial situation by gaining additional state support and loans. There is some more focus on the future, and limited effort to develop plans beyond the time of the pandemic; but because nobody has the faintest idea how long that will last, it is minor adjustments to products and services that dominate. In essence, from a resource-based perspective, the choices made by our respondents are limited to the building of operational rather than strategic capabilities to enable their firms to survive.

Third, our study sheds light on the managerial sense-making that becomes a major moderator of companies' adaptive changes in pandemic times. Our research reveals that many managers try to give personal meaning to the situation of discontinuity they face. For some people, this is an opportunity to acquire new competences – e.g. in the area of e-commerce, or managing a virtual organization. Others appreciate the sense of agency, the fact that they feel 'needed' by people in the organization, the possibility of using crisis-management skills, better organization of their own work, or discovering unrealized resources of strength, determination and creativity. But for many, the pandemic also becomes a special time of reflection, providing for a recognition of personal values *("I noticed what is important to me, and what I can live without")*, a confrontation with the image of former authorities and a development of autonomy of action *("I discovered that there are no mentors, leaders who would be the pillars on which one could base or take a pattern. And this belief (...) gave me inner peace and motivation to look for my own way. This is a new discovery for me.")*, with new plans then formulated, and – most importantly – the acceptance that situations are simply *"beyond our control"*.

A reflective attitude then seems to become a 'shield', increasing managerial resilience in the pandemic era, and moderating the sense of urgency to make changes or adaptations that are not absolutely necessary. As one respondent noted, *"Peace is coming back to me. An unreasonable one, not one that results from controlling the situation. Rather, it comes from accepting the inevitability of change and the need to face it... I would like to go through this crisis and become a bit-wiser person"*.

Our findings are tempered by three limitations. First, due to the unique pandemic conditions, we decided to use a convenience sample of former alumni of EMBA programs that are CEOs or members of Executive Boards of their companies. This is then a biased sample in terms of representativeness for the Polish economy, but we believe it offers a reasonable approximation of the behaviors of professional managers. Second, it is biased sample in terms of the business situations of responding companies. Most (70 %) of them are – in spite of all the difficulties and disruptions – actually coping reasonably well with the pandemic conditions. That said, we have no reason to believe that managers from companies in dire straits would have had perspectives or emotions very different from those our respondents manifest. The pandemic situation is very new and difficult for all companies.

Third, while the four-month timespan of our study is rather short for a longitudinal research project, we maintain that, with all the limitations, it still offers an important insight into managerial cognitions, emotions and actions, given it encompasses three major environmental jolts, i.e. the pandemic outbreak, the imposition of state lockdown in Poland, and a period of restriction-lifting that proved premature in light of the pandemic's comeback in November and December 2020.

Acknowledgements

We appreciate the support of Kozminski University (research grant number 908.2.6).

References

Cameron, E./Green, M. (2020): Making sense of change management, 5th ed. London: Kogan Page.

Christensen, C. M. (2013): The innovator's dilemma: when new technologies cause great firms to fail. Harvard: Harvard Business Review Press.

Ciszewska-Mlinarič, M., Obloj, K., Wąsowska, A. (2018): Internationalisation choices of Polish firms during the post-socialism transition period: The role of institutional conditions at firm's foundation, in: Business History, 60, 562–600.

CMSG (Centrum Monitoringu Sytuacji Gospodarczej) (2020): The economic situation of businesses in the coronavirus era (in Polish), access: https://pracodawcyrp.pl/aktualnosci-koronawirus/badanie-cmsg-sytuacja-ekonomiczna-przedsiebiorstw-w-czasach-koronawirusa-wrocil-sceptycyzm

Gehman, J./Glaser, V.L./Eisenhardt, K.M./Gioia, D.A./Langley, A./Corley, K.G. (2018): Finding theory-method fit: A comparison of three qualitative approaches to theory building, in: Journal of Management Inquiry, 27, 3, 284–300.

Gioia, D.A./Corley, K.G./Hamilton, A.L. (2013): Seeking qualitative rigor in inductive research: Notes on the Gioia methodology, in: Organizational Research Methods, 16, 1, 15–31.

Glaser, B./Strauss, A. (1999): The discovery of grounded theory: Strategies for qualitative research. Aldine: Transaction.
March, J.G. (1981): Footnotes to organizational change, in: Administrative Science Quarterly, 26, 4, 563–577.
Meyer, A.D./Brooks, G.R./Goes, J.B. (1990): Environmental jolts and industry revolutions: organizational responses to discontinuous change, in: Strategic Management Journal, 11, Special Issue, 93–110.
Micelotta, E./Lounsbury, M./Greenwood, R. (2017): Pathways of institutional change: An integrative review and research agenda, in: Journal of Management, 43, 6, 1885–1910.
Navigator Capital Group (2020): Companies in the Age of COVID-19 (in Polish), access: https://pracodawcyrp.pl/upload/files/2020/06/navigator-capital-group-raport-z-badania-firm-2020-1.pdf
Obloj, T./Obloj, K./Pratt, M. G. (2010): Dominant logic and entrepreneurial firms 'performance in a transition economy, in: Entrepreneurship Theory and Practice, 34, 1, 151–170.
PwC (2020): Polish micro, small and medium sized enterprises in the face of the COVID 19 pandemic, access: https://www.pwc.com/c1/future-of-government-cee/covid19/assessing-the-impact-of-covid-19.html
Schilke, O. (2014): On the contingent value of dynamic capabilities for competitive advantage: The nonlinear moderating effect of environmental dynamism, in: Strategic Management Journal, 35, 2, 179–203.
Teece, D. J./Pisano, G./Shuen, A. (1997): Dynamic capabilities and strategic management, in: Strategic Management Journal, 18, 7, 509–533
Tsoukas, H./Chia, R. (2002): An organizational becoming: Rethinking organizational change, in: Organization Science, 13, 5, 567–582.
Tushman, M.L./Anderson, P. (1986): Technological discontinuities and organizational environments, in: Administrative Science Quarterly, 31, 3, 439–465.
Van de Ven, A.H./Poole, S.M. (1995): Explaining development and change in organization, in: Academy of Management Review, 20, 3, 510–540.

Appendix 1. The questionnaire

1. *When did the first business disruptions appear in the environment, or in your company, as a result of the pandemic?*
2. *What was the nature of these disturbances?*
3. *Which of these disruptions in the last 2 weeks has had the most significant impact for business? Why?*
4. *Which of these disruptions has become less important in the past 2 weeks? Why?*
5. *What are the main criteria you follow when taking anti-crisis measures?*
6. *What anti-crisis measures did you take in March, from the moment you decided to react?*
7. *Which of the actions taken so far do you consider the most important and effective? Why?*

8. Which of the actions taken turned out to be less important and effective? Why?
9. Overall – how do you feel you are coping with the pandemic challenge so far? Why?

Questions added in the second and third rounds:
10. Do you make plans that go beyond the pandemic time, beyond the "here and now" horizon?
11. How has your company's relationships with key stakeholders (suppliers, customers, competitors) and their importance changed during the pandemic? Are they more cooperative or conflicting? Have you taken any joint action?
12. What are the moods (emotions) of people in your company at the moment? Why?
13. How do you evaluate Polish state administration support programs ('shields')? Why?

Exploration and Exploitation of Nascent Local Business Opportunities during the Global Disruption: Strategic Actions of Subsidiaries of Large Multinational IT Corporations in Russia in the period of the COVID-19 Pandemic[*]

Ivan Shchetinin, Sergey Lapshin[**]

Abstract

This paper discusses the strategic actions taken by the Russian subsidiaries of two large multinational information technology (IT) corporations during the COVID-19 pandemic. These companies faced explosive growth in local demand for hardware and IT solutions due to the increased digitalization of business and greater emphasis on remote working during the lockdown. The management of the Russian subsidiaries demonstrated great ingenuity in redesigning business processes and acquiring additional resources to satisfy the growing demand. As a result, the performance of the Russian subsidiaries radically improved during 2020; however, some of the implemented strategic actions were not welcomed by the corporate headquarters as they required amendment of the existing subsidiary mandates.

Keywords: pandemic, strategic actions, multinational corporations, IT sector, subsidiary mandates
JEL Codes: F23; L21; L86

1. Introduction

According to data from the United Nations Conference on Trade and Development (UNCTAD), the flow of foreign direct investment into the Russian economy has been extremely volatile since 2008 (UNCTAD 2020). The year 2013 witnessed the highest amount of investment inflows, of more than US $ 53 billion. The two-fold fall of the local currency at the end of 2014 was a major blow to foreign direct investment in Russia, but in 2019, there was an almost threefold increase in the volume of investments compared to 2015.

Since 2014, the activities of 'western' companies (companies from developed economies) in Russia have been affected by sanctions, which have resulted in four key problems:

---

[*] Received: 28.12.20, Accepted: 6.1.21, 0 revisions.
[**] *Ivan Shchetinin (corresponding author),* Ph.D student, Department of Strategic and International Management, Higher School of Economics. Email: ivan.shchetinin@gmail.com. Main research interests: international management, strategic management, corporate venture capital, corporate investments.
Sergey Lapshin, Junior Research Fellow, Department of Strategic and International Management, Higher School of Economics. Email: lap-leonid@yandex.ru. Main research interests: strategic organizational design, headquarter-subsidiary relationships, international management, strategic management.

- growing difficulty in maintaining the loyalty of foreign businesses operating in Russia to both the country of origin and Russian authorities,
- rapidly deteriorating quality of the government's regulatory efforts,
- self-imposed Russian embargo on imports of foodstuff from the USA and EU, and on the use of foreign technologies in key governmental organizations (August 2014), and
- economic recession caused by the fall in oil prices and government revenues.

Nevertheless, from 2012 to 2018, more than 260 new enterprises were established by foreign investors in Russia (Gurkov et al. 2020). By the end of 2019 (prior to the outbreak of the COVID-19 pandemic), foreign companies occupied important positions in the Russian economy:

- 40 subsidiaries of foreign corporations had Russian sales over US $ 1 Billion.
- Subsidiaries of foreign corporations controlled 100 % of domestic cigarette production, 80 % of car assembly (including contract manufacturing), 60–70 % of production in different food segments, 50 % of production of road building equipment, 50 % of production of special chemicals, 40 % of production of pharmaceuticals, and 30 % of production of construction materials (Gurkov et al. 2020).
- Besides, subsidiaries of foreign corporations occupied important positions in different types of services (IT services, banking, insurance, business real estate etc.).

The pandemic has seriously affected most sectors of the Russian economy with a significant presence of foreign companies. However, the impact of the pandemic has been quite heterogeneous in different sectors. While overall demand for most goods and services has declined, several business areas such as information technology (IT), pharmaceuticals, medical equipment, and online commerce have experienced tremendous growth in Russia since the beginning of the pandemic, like in most other countries (McKibbin et al. 2020). The pandemic has also improved the attitudes of the Russian government towards local subsidiaries of western, especially US, corporations in IT. Since 2014, western IT companies in Russia have been experiencing challenges mainly due to an aggressive import substitution policy for hardware and software. Global IT vendors such as Dell, Hewlett Packard Enterprise, and Oracle faced new restrictions on their business activities in Russia, especially in terms of access to government-backed orders, which were given to local and Chinese companies. Such restrictions were more severe in terms of supply of hardware but less so for IT services. Thus, the business of service-based IT companies experienced growth, and western IT companies had to increase their Russian subsidiaries' number of employees and overall competence in IT services. The pandemic created an absolute shortage of both IT hardware and software in the local market and de-facto lifted many restrictions on the operation of western IT companies in Russia.

This paper discusses, in detail, the strategic actions taken by the Russian subsidiaries of two major global IT companies, which successfully met the explosive growth in demand from local companies for hardware, software, and complex IT solutions. This helped equip the drastically increased number of distant workplaces, and meet the critical need of local corporations in different sectors for the digitalization of business transactions.

The rest of the paper is organized as follows. In the next two sections, we present the theoretical framework of the study and the research methodology. Then, we present the cases themselves. The discussion section contains some reflections on the abilities of peripheral subsidiaries to cope with radical changes in the business environment. The conclusions indicate promising avenues for further studies.

2. Theoretical framework of the study

For the present study, we construct a theoretical framework that is suitable for describing situations when 'peripheral subsidiaries' face unique local opportunities for growth. Specifically, we consider the 'behavioural theory of the multinational corporation' (Birkinshaw 1995, 1996; Aharoni 2010, Ciabuschi et al. 2011; Ciabuschi et al. 2012; Conroy/Collings 2016; Bouquet et al. 2016; ul Haq et al. 2017; Verbeke/Yuan, 2020), which is a more appropriate framework for describing such situations.

Within this approach, the position of a subsidiary in the corporate business portfolio is determined not only by 'objective' factors (the share of a subsidiary's revenue and net cash flow in the total revenues and cash flows of the corporate parent, the absolute and relative performance of the subsidiary, the volatility of performance indicators, and the ability to repatriate value from a subsidiary) but also by a set of behavioural elements—the psychic distance of indigenous subsidiary managers from top corporate executives and, relatedly, the level of trust and empathy between corporate headquarters and a subsidiary's managers, as well as attitudes towards indigenous business practices (which can be considered as acceptable, hardly acceptable, or completely inappropriate by the corporate parent), among others. As suggested by (Aharoni et al., 2011: 137–138), such attitudes can be expressed not by a single corporate executive but be the dominant attitudes of top management teams serving as collective decision-makers. The lack of trust and empathy of the top management team of the corporate parent, coupled with objective difficulties associated with value appropriation, bring even a well-performing subsidiary into the 'corporate periphery'. This means that such subsidiaries encounter stricter control on operations, meagre development budgets, and low opportunities for rewards and promotion of indigenous managers.

As a result, a peripheral subsidiary usually lacks the necessary resources to exploit nascent business opportunities and thus, looks to the corporate headquarters for additional resources. According to Verbeke and Yuan (2020), decisions at the corporate headquarters may largely depend on the inclinations of individual members of a top management team, who may be driven by a variety of motivations and have different abilities. Thus, motivations and abilities together determine whether corporate executives will choose to intervene in subsidiary initiatives and the effectiveness of such intervention. The motives of corporate executives can vary in degree and direction, ranging from a 'good cause' rationale (Williamson 1996) to pursuing personal private interests while putting on an appearance of serious managerial activity in relation to a subsidiary (Forsgren 2015). Thus, previous research suggests that multinational corporations (MNCs) will not always react to changes in the external environment and new opportunities in accordance with the resource-based view.

Gurkov et al. (2018) and Gurkov (2019) demonstrate that Russian subsidiaries of western multinational corporations experience 'peripherization' regardless of their current performance and the growth perspectives of the business segments in which they operate. This is due to higher restrictions on value repatriation, low trust and empathy towards indigenous managers, and the resulting higher costs of monitoring the subsidiary's operations.

Therefore, we postulate the following flow of events when peripheral subsidiaries face unexpected growth of demand in their business domains:

1) Local subsidiaries will try to explore and exploit nascent business opportunities especially if the additional demand for their goods or services is presented in a 'pull' manner.
2) As the proper exploitation of the nascent business opportunities may require additional resources beyond the pool of resources available to subsidiaries, they will turn to the corporate headquarters for 'emergency resource re-employment'.
3) Initially, such calls from the corporate periphery will be met with 'sheer ignorance' (using the words of (Chiabuchi et al. 2012)), the resources finally allocated to subsidiaries may be unsatisfactory.
4) If the amount of resources provided by the corporate parent is unsatisfactory, subsidiaries will try to try to explore local substitutes; such actions may be beyond the existing subsidiaries' mandate and also alter the established modes of operations.
5) With sufficient ingenuity in finding and utilizing local resources, there are greater probabilities that subsidiaries will successfully exploit the nascent

business opportunities, maintaining or even improving their performance and strengthening their positions in their business domains.

3. Research methods

Our research approach is based on a comparison of two cases of quite similar Russian subsidiaries of western multinational corporations. Studies based on a small number of cases of similar companies are useful for exploring new phenomena, and for exploring, illustrating, and developing theory (Siggelkow 2007; Yin 2009). Such studies can illustrate conceptual frameworks and highlight the need for new lenses to explore phenomena (Lervik 2011). For example, in Vaara et al. (2005), which dealt with the power implications of corporate language policies, the role of the case was to illustrate a phenomenon and motivate the search for alternative lenses in order to move beyond episodic notions of power in MNCs. Müller at al., (2018) used the cases of Google an Yahoo to present a specific form of business model innovation. A study based on a small number of similar cases balances depth and generalizability through systematic comparisons across cases (Ragin 1987), thus contributing to further rigorous theory development (Eisenhardt 1989). In addition, Aharoni (2011, 47) insightfully noted that the case study is well suited for identifying and further researching 'black swans' because of its in-depth approach.

The use of cases of two similar Russian subsidiaries of multinational corporations has several additional advantages. First, they present the features of the development of an important sector (IT) in a large Eastern European economy during the pandemic. Second, the comparison of the cases assists to reveal both common and company-specific elements of strategic actions of subsidiaries of western IT companies during the pandemic. Third, as was demonstrated by Gurkov (2015), "a subsidiary's view" may reveal a lot about the corporate parenting style of the corporate parent.

For both cases in this study, we use action research. Both authors were directly involved in the design and implementation of most measures related to the amendment of business operations, including working on the subsidiary's action plans and other formal documents, participating in different working meetings, and making occasional contact with important local clients. In addition, informal communications with the senior managers of the Russian subsidiaries enabled the authors to obtain first-hand information about the dynamics of headquarters–subsidiary relations during the pandemic.

4. The Cases

In this section, we present the cases of the Russian divisions of two western IT companies, with combined global revenues exceeding US $ 106 billion, which we will call Alpha and Beta. Alpha and Beta are similar in many ways. Both corporations are more than 70 years old, and both initially emerged as producers of computational machinery before diversifying to IT services. One corporation still combines the production of hardware infrastructure products with IT services; the second company combines some niche highly specialized computer manufacturing with IT and business services, including cloud computing and artificial intelligence solutions.

4.1 Alpha Company

The Russian division of Alpha began Financial Year (FY) 2020, which commenced on November 1, 2019, on the cusp of major changes. First, the results of 2019 were noticeably lower than a year earlier—the Football World Cup in Russia in 2018 had provided new business opportunities and led to a spike in short-term business projects. Second, the parent company undertook a reallocation of country subsidiaries between different regional headquarters. In 2018–2019, the Russian subsidiary was a part of the 'elite region' DACHR, which historically comprised three countries: Germany, Austria, and Switzerland. DACH (without Russia) was the second-largest contributor to the parent company's revenues. Accordingly, the region was part of the 'corporate core', and corporate executives were receptive to the wishes of the regional headquarters. It should be noted that in DACHR, the share of Russian business in the total revenues was around 20 %, similar to that of Switzerland.

In FY 2020, Russia was expected to move to the newly formed CERTA region (Central and Eastern Europe, Russia, Turkey, and Africa without South Africa). This region combined peripheral subsidiaries to facilitate stronger control of these subsidiaries' operations, while allowing little managerial discretion on several operational issues. The share of Russian business in the total revenues was now approximately 31 %.

Thus, there was a classic movement of the unit from the 'core' to the periphery. The transition had several effects on the Russian subsidiary:

– The global headquarters became less inclined to listen to the country managers.
– Expenses on business trips and international business meetings were reduced.
– There was an increase in the share of 'low-touch business' (services in which a significant part of activities was mostly performed by independents local contractors) to decrease the total payroll expenses of the Russian subsidiary.
– New requirements were imposed on the gross margin of operations, with the target set to a new level that was 6 % higher compared to the previous year. This was done despite tough competition in most business segments.
– Reduced marketing budgets limited personal encounters with potential clients—a must for corporate sales in Russia.

The subsidiary's management had to accept the new circumstances but was uncertain about meeting the newly imposed performance targets.

February 2020 marked the beginning of a worldwide outbreak of COVID-19, which was undoubtedly a tragedy but also created unexpected opportunities for the IT sector worldwide. Alpha's subsidiary in Russia was fully compliant with the Russian government's requirement that companies enable remote work for a proportion of their employees; however, the company was also lucky in that the law exempted companies in the IT segment from the complete lockdown that was imposed in Russia from March 28 to April 30, 2020.

Many large local companies faced the urgent need to create infrastructure to enable remote working, as restrictions on the physical appearance of employees in offices continued even after the lockdown. As a company with a 'traditional IT infrastructure' background, Alpha offered a variety of different IT equipment (such as servers, networking equipment, and data storage systems). This became critical during the pandemic, which had necessitated an immediate and significant transition to distant work and the establishment of appropriate supporting infrastructure. Moreover, in recent years, the company had been actively developing a department specializing in technology consulting, which undertakes, in particular, projects for turn-key installation of modern IT infrastructure for large local companies.

When the lockdown was implemented, there was great demand for standard equipment that was already stored in distributors' warehouses, whereas the demand for customized equipment dropped sharply. As a result, the importance of the services department, which was able to create customized solutions based on standard equipment, greatly increased. Additional revenues from tuning the standard equipment counterbalanced the drop in sales of customized equipment and increased the gross margin of operations, while keeping the total revenue stable.

The management of the Russian subsidiary of Alpha took another important decision—to soften the pricing policy. As most of their local clients faced the same emergency situation because of the lockdown, the company reduced the demand for advance payments as well as allowed late final payments; moreover, the prices of various services were decreased and some services were offered to customers at nominal prices.

That policy affected the gross margin from operations and the headquarters quickly forbade both payment delays and discounts to local customers. The subsidiary had no choice but to adopt the headquarters' policy, but it quickly implemented other measures to help their customers, such as making greater use of subcontracts. Local IT firms were invited to perform a greater part of the overall work. Thus, the direct contract with Alpha was reconfigured to include only a share of operations with higher gross margins; the remaining operations were arranged as separate contracts with local IT firms, which set lower prices and offered a comparable level of service quality.

Another challenge faced by the Russian subsidiary was the corporate-wide initiative to launch a new version of a product. The Russian IT market is very conservative; therefore, the news that the current system would be phased out in June 2020 was met with discontent. Most local customers were not ready to switch to a new version of the product before November–December 2020, when the budgets of the IT departments of local firms are set. The Russian subsidiary was extremely concerned about the launch, but was powerless in postponing the corporate-wide initiative as an exception for Russia. Fortunately for the subsidiary, the worldwide problems with components delayed the global release of the new system. The Russian subsidiary announced that product discontinuance was officially delayed, creating a rush in demand for the old product, which had to be purchased and entirely paid for before the end of the year in order to be installed later.

The results show that the actions implemented by the Russian subsidiary achieved undisputed success with respect to resilience and performance in 2020.

– It achieved 98 % of the initially projected revenues set in September 2019 (the projection of revenues was not adjusted during the pandemic).
– The revenue of the Russian division in US$ terms grew from 30 % to 41 % of the total revenue of the CERTA region.
– The gross margin from operations increased from 18 % in 2019 to 25.5 % in 2020, 1.3 % higher than the initial (already elevated) target.

The growth in sales could have been even more spectacular. However, the Russian subsidiary of Alpha ran out of stock (Chinese and Taiwan factories were closed because of the pandemic, and it was impossible to relocate the stock to other geographical areas due to several organizational and technical reasons).

However, during the award ceremony for CERTA countries, Russia was not selected as a winner.

4.2 Beta Company

In this section, we describe the situation in the Russian subsidiary of the second corporation. During the COVID-19 pandemic and the quarter with the most stringent lockdown in Russia (stoppage of most enterprises and construction projects, closure of transport links between countries, and even restrictions on the free movement of people between and inside regions), the Russian subsidiary of Beta Corporation showed almost double-digit growth in revenue in all business segments and signed a record volume of new contracts; for some segments, there was a triple-digit growth in signed contracts. However, despite the impressive results, the subsidiary faced a serious challenge. The subsidiary was in the process of designing and signing a new contract, which would have been the biggest project in the history of the subsidiary. The deal would have ensured profitable functioning of the whole subsidiary for two years. However, the client put forth one condition for signing the contract – the deferral of the first contract payment until the end of first quarter of 2021. From the perspective of the financial department of the parent company, the contract would have resulted in negative gross profit in one quarter, which was unacceptable for contracts of that size. The rigid financial control applied to the Russian subsidiary did not allow for any exceptions. The only possibility for the local subsidiary was to apply for an internal loan from the corporate treasury. The application was rejected. The management of the subsidiary was told that the practice of internal loans was applicable for all countries in which Beta was present, except for Russia, where such loans were banned two years ago. The subsidiary's management, trying to save the deal, suggested to the headquarters the option of obtaining a loan from a Russian commercial bank. However, this idea was also rejected as the headquarters did not wish to bear additional risks. Moreover, another consideration emerged – to fulfil the contract, a major increase in headcount was necessary. The corporate headquarters did not allow hiring of people before contract being signed and asked the subsidiary to postpone all additional staffing until the contract was finally signed. The subsidiary managers found a solution by offering part-time employment to the staff of sister subsidiaries (especially, Ukraine). The solution presented a win-win situation:

– The Russian subsidiary's management liked this practice because it gave them the opportunity to choose the best employees, while avoiding additional recruitment costs and saving on labour costs, since the wages in Ukraine are lower than in Russia.
– The employees liked it, as working on a large contact increased their employability.
– The management of the sister subsidiary liked it because their employees achieved a higher utilization rate, and this improved some key performance indicators (KPIs) imposed by the corporate headquarters on the subsidiary's management.

As a result, the Russian division of the Beta corporation faced in December 2020 the following situation:

1) creation of macro regions by combining small geographic markets into large clusters at the level of organizational design;
2) significant reduction in investment and development plans;
3) restrictions on staff recruitment, even to compensate for the natural turnover of staff;

4) tightening control systems (complicating the process of negotiating transactions, increasing the time period of the approval cycle, generating higher costs, etc.);
5) reduction of budgets for managers;
6) deprivation of the possibility to approach financial lenders for transactions with deferred payments (which are necessary in the COVID era, when customers are demanding that work begin as soon as possible, and payment be deferred); and
7) despite the subsidiary's best efforts, several problems remain unresolved, impeding the efficient exploitation of nascent market opportunities.

5. Discussion

In general, the postulated flow of events has been proven. Both subsidiaries demonstrated high agility in redesigning existing operations; ingenuity in obtaining the necessary additional resources (either by cooperation with local firms or closer cooperation with sister subsidiaries); and several elements of ambidexterity. Despite facing a spike in demand for their goods and services, both subsidiaries did not use 'predatory pricing', but instead, tried to keep the prices and payment conditions favourable to local clients, expecting the continuation of business relationships with them after the pandemic. Unfortunately, such elements of ambidextrous behaviour were not properly understood and supported by the corporate headquarters. In both the described cases, the headquarters did not consider the pandemic a valid reason for changing operational plans and amending subsidiaries' mandate. We should stress that at the end of 2014, when facing the twofold devaluation of the local currency, the western corporations in Russia demonstrated higher flexibility and wider repertoire of strategic actions (see Gurkov, 2016).

We speculate that the problem of rapid and unexpected devaluation of the local currency is a familiar matter for major multinational corporations (sudden devaluations of local currency occur frequently in emerging markets), and the corporate headquarters has an established procedure for dealing with such situations; by contrast, the pandemic presented a pure 'black swan' (completely unexpected event with no precedents) event. The corporate headquarters had neither corporate-wide emergency plans ready for such situations nor established procedures to guide subsidiaries' actions. In such situation both Russian subsidiaries had neither direct power to amend some corporate policies nor time to engage into complicated and usually time-consuming corporate politics (see Geppert and Dorrebacher 2014). Following the model presented by Dorrembacher and Gammelgaard (2016), both Russian subsidiaries were in high resource dependency from the headquarters and put insufficient efforts in calls for resources, so many subsidiaries' initiatives were rejected or accepted as interim measures.

Moreover, as was indicated by Merendino and Sarens (2020), the problem of behaviour patterns rigidity of corporate headquarters during the pandemic might lay above – in the board of directors of the corporate parents. According to (Merendino/Sarens 2020, 415), "…directors have a selective perception of the environment, resulting in a filtered and narrowed vision of a crisis; this explains why boards often lack proactivity in crisis detection and response", and therefore restrict both the repertoire of actions and the speed of changes of actions of corporate headquarters.

6. Conclusions and suggestions for further studies

Our evaluation of the strategic actions of the Russian subsidiaries of two similar global IT companies demonstrates the subsidiaries' agility and ambidexterity. It also reflects the high level of isomorphism in the negative reaction of corporate headquarters to actions that potentially exceeded the subsidiaries' prescribed mandates. We speculate that such situations may be typical in many subsidiaries of western multinational corporations not only in Russia, but also in other East European countries where a large share of country subsidiaries are viewed by their parent companies as being on the 'corporate periphery'. Testing that proposition may be a promising avenue for further research.

Acknowledgements

The authors wish to thank the editor of the special issue, Prof. Thomas Steger, Prof Monika Wieczorek-Kosmala and Prof. Igor Gurkov, whose valuable suggestions helped us to improve the paper.

References

Aharoni, Y. (2010). Behavioral elements in foreign direct investments, in: Advances in International Management, 23, 73–111, Bingley: Emerald

Aharoni, Y. (2011). Fifty years of case research in international business: The power of outliers and black swans, in: Piekkari, R. and Welch, C. (Eds.). Rethinking the Case Study in International Business and Management Research, 41–54, Cheltenham: Edward Elgar.

Aharoni, Y./Tihanyi, L./Connelly, B.L. (2011). Managerial decision-making in international business: A forty-five-year retrospective, in Journal of World Business, 46, 135–142

Birkinshaw, J. (1995). Entrepreneurship in multinational corporations: the initiative process in foreign subsidiaries. Unpublished doctoral dissertation, Western Business School, University of Western Ontario.

Birkinshaw, J. (1996). How multinational subsidiary mandates are gained and lost, in: Journal of International Business Studies, 27, 3, 467–495.

Bouquet, C./Birkinshaw, J./Barsous, J. (2016). Fighting the "headquarters knows best" syndrome, in: MIT Sloan Management Review, 57, 2, 58–66

Ciabuschi, F./Forsgren, M./Martín, O.M. (2011). Rationality vs. ignorance: the role of MNE headquarters in subsidiaries' innovation processes, in: Journal of International Business Studies, 50, 4, 112–124.

Ciabuschi, F./Forsgren, M./Martín, O.M. (2012). Headquarters involvement and efficiency of innovation development and transfer in multinationals: a matter of sheer ignorance?, in: International Business Review, 21, 2, 130–144

Conroy, K./Collings, D. (2016). The legitimacy of subsidiary issue selling: balancing positive and negative attention from corporate headquarters, in: Journal of World Business, 51, 4, 612–627.

Dorrenbacher, C./Gammelgaard, J. (2016). Subsidiary initiative taking in multinational corporations: The relationship between power and issue selling, in: Organization Studies, 37, 9, 1249–1270.

Eisenhardt, K.M. (1989). Building theory from case study research, in: Academy of Management Review, 14, 4, 532–550.

Forsgren, M. (2015). The 'parenting advantage' and innovation processes in the multinational firm: does top management mess things up? In: Transnational Corporations and Transnational Governance. Palgrave Macmillan, London, 97–111.

Geppert, M./Dorrenbacher, C. (2014). Politics and power within multinational corporations: Mainstream studies, emerging critical approaches and suggestions for future research, in: International Journal of Management Reviews, 16, 226–244.

Gurkov, I. (2015). Corporate parenting styles of the multinational corporation: A subsidiary view. In: R.Van Tulder, A.Verbeke, R. Drogendijk (Eds.). The Future of Global Organizing. Progress in International Business Research, 10. Emerald, Bingley, 57–78.

Gurkov, I. (2016). Against the wind – new factories of Russian manufacturing subsidiaries of Western multinational corporations, in: Eurasian Geography and Economics, 57, 2, 161–179

Gurkov, I. (2019). The growing anisotropy of the multinational corporation in the "new normal", in: Journal of Organizational Change Management, 32, 2, 194–207.

Gurkov, I./Kokorina, A./Lapshin, S./Saidov, Z./Balaeva, O. (2020). Foreign direct investment in a stagnant economy: Recent experience of FDI in manufacturing facilities in Russia, in Journal of East-West Business, 26, 2, 109–130

Gurkov, I./Morgunov, E./Saidov, Z./Arshavsky, A. (2018). Perspectives of manufacturing subsidiaries of foreign companies in Russia: Frontier, faubourg or sticks?, in: Foresight and STI Governance, 12, 2, 24–35.

Lervik, J. E. B. (2011). The single MNC as a research site, In: R.Pekkari, C.Welsh (Eds). Rethinking the case study in international business and management research, Cheltenham, Edward Elgar, 229–250.

McKibbin, W./Fernando, R. (2020). The Global Macroeconomic Impacts of COVID-19: Seven Scenarios, in: CAMA Working Paper.

Merendino, A./Sarens, G. (2020). Crisis? What crisis? Exploring the cognitive constraints on boards of directors in times of uncertainty, in Journal of Business Research, 118, 415–430.

Müller, C.N./Kijl, B./Visnjic, I. (2018). Envelopment lessons to manage digital platforms: The cases of Google and Yahoo, in: Strategic Change, 27, 2, 139–149

Ragin, C.C. (1987). The Comparative Method: Moving Beyond Qualitative and Quantitative Strategies, Berkeley and Los Angeles, CA: University of California Press.

Siggelkow, N. (2007). Persuasion with case studies, in: Academy of Management Journal, 50, 1, 20–24.

UNCTAD (2020). World Investment Report – International Production Beyond the Pandemic. Geneva, UNCTAD.

Vaara, E./ Tienari, J./ Piekkari, R./. Säntti, R. (2005). Language and the circuits of power in a merging multinational corporation, in: Journal of Management Studies, 42, 3, 595–623.

Verbeke, A./Yuan, W. (2020). The tyranny of the head office? Revisiting corporate headquarters'(CHQs) role in MNE subsidiary initiatives, in: Journal of Organization Design, 9, 1, 2.

Williamson, O.E. (1996). The mechanisms of governance, in: Oxford University Press, Oxford, UK.

Yin, R.K. (2009). Case Study Research: Design and Methods, 4th edn, Thousand Oaks, CA: Sage.

Human Resource Management during the COVID-19 Pandemic: Evidence from Armenia[*]

Mane Beglaryan, Vache Gabrielyan, Gayane Shakhmuradyan[**]

Abstract

The paper examines human resource management during the initial phases of the COVID-19 pandemic in Armenia. It is hypothesised that professionals have made a smoother transition to remote work than non-professionals, and industry has a significant impact on remote work during the pandemic. Additionally, we discuss whether small and medium enterprises have been able to reorganise operations faster than larger enterprises. Survey data analyses fully support the first and second hypotheses, but only partially support the third. The findings suggest that public investment in digital infrastructures, as well as private investment in employee training and development, would be the most effective ways to withstand future pandemic crises.

Keywords: COVID-19 pandemic, economic crisis, human resource management, private enterprises, remote work
JEL Codes: J50, M12, M54

1. Introduction

Originating in China in December 2019, the COVID-19 pandemic has come to constitute a global health crisis unprecedented in decades (World Health Organisation 2021). Restrictions on individual movement and closure of non-essential businesses, mandated by governments to curb the spread of the disease, have caused disruptions in economic activity worldwide, thus bringing about an unprecedented global economic crisis (International Monetary Fund 2021; World Bank 2021). Business management, and particularly human resource management, are among the most affected by the current crisis, as it has been characterised by temporary and permanent closures of production and sales sites, transition to remote work and e-commerce, as well as employee layoffs and pay reduction (Carnevale/Hatak 2020; International Labour Organisation

---

[*] Received: 11.1.21, Accepted: 3.3.21, 2 revisions.
[**] *Mane Beglaryan,* Associate Professor, MBA Program Chair, College of Business and Economics, American University of Armenia. Email: mbeglaryan@aua.am. Main research interests: strategic human resource management, entrepreneurship, organisational culture and learning, organisational resilience, small and medium enterprises.
Vache Gabrielyan, Professor, Dean, College of Business and Economics, American University of Armenia. Email: vache.gabrielyan@aua.am. Main research interests: public administration, organisational management and theory, macroeconomics.
Gayane Shakhmuradyan, Teaching Associate, Research Assistant, College of Business and Economics, American University of Armenia. Email: gayane_shakhmuradyan19@alumni.aua.am. Main research interests: social and economic policy, public finance, development economics.

2021; Organisation for Economic Co-operation and Development 2021; Verma/Gustafsson 2020).

Most observers underscore that COVID-19 has accelerated the pace of workplace digitisation, and changes in the organisation of work induced by it will persist long after the health and economic repercussions are overcome (Bartik et al. 2020 a; Caligiuri et al. 2020; LaBerge et al. 2020). However, the ability of private enterprises to implement remote work practices under the pandemic has not been uniform: factors such as the industry of operations and the skillset of the employees have greatly determined the business ability to transition to online (Bartik et al. 2020 a; Brynjolfsson et al. 2020; del Rio-Chanona et al. 2020). This paper aims to contribute to the literature on human resource management during the pandemic by examining remote work in Armenian private enterprises. The case of Armenia is interesting, as the level of workplace digitisation is not high as compared to developed and other developing economies (Saltiel 2020), but there seems to be variability in the ability of enterprises of different size (i.e., small and medium vs. large) to cope with the pandemic (Beglaryan/Shakhmuradyan 2020).

The paper is structured as follows: in the next section, the literature on the economic impact of the pandemic and human resource management under it is reviewed, and hypotheses relevant to private enterprises in Armenia are advanced. The third and fourth sections elaborate on the research methodology and data analysis, respectively. The fifth section discusses the main findings and policy implications, while a final section concludes.

2. Literature Review and Hypotheses

COVID-19, the disease caused by the novel coronavirus, has come to constitute a global pandemic since March 2020 (World Health Organisation 2021). A crisis of social nature, the pandemic has had immense economic repercussions, bringing about temporary and permanent closures of private enterprises and massive layoffs (International Labour Organisation 2021; World Bank 2021). The recent (October 2020 and January 2021) updates of the International Monetary Fund's *World Economic Outlook* suggest that there has been progress in overcoming the effects of the pandemic since April 2020, especially as vaccines have been approved, but recovery is slow due to partial or full reinstalment of lockdowns in many countries considering the renewed waves and variants of the disease (International Monetary Fund 2021).

To maintain continuity of operations during the pandemic, business enterprises have introduced and implemented remote work practices: the fundamental aspects of human resource management (HRM), including recruitment, selection, training, and performance appraisal, have been reorganised in line with the 'new normal', i.e., remote work (Bailey/Breslin 2021; Carnevale/Hatak 2020). As noted by Agarwal (2021), during a crisis like COVID-19, employee-centred HRM practices and an agile HRM system that support personal and family life are more relevant and effective. However, the extent of implementation of remote work practices has not been even across different occupations and industries. Several studies on the impact of the pandemic suggest that high-wage occupations (managers and professionals) are less affected by the pandemic than low-wage occupations (manual work, clerical, and administrative jobs) due to their ability to work remotely (Bartik et al. 2020a; Brynjolfsson et al. 2020; del Rio-Chanona et al. 2020; Dingel/Neiman 2020; Gabrielyan 2020; Saltiel 2020). The same strand of research emphasises that employees of industries in which work can be carried out remotely, e.g. information and communications, finance and insurance, professional and scientific work, and education, have made a transition to remote work during the pandemic, while their counterparts in industries requiring interpersonal contact, e.g. tourism, hospitality, and transportation, have been laid off or furloughed (Bartik et al. 2020a; Béland et al. 2020; del Rio-Chanona et al. 2020; Dingel/Neiman 2020). In light of this evidence, we hypothesise that

Hypothesis 1: *Professionals have made a smoother transition to remote work during the pandemic than non-professionals.*[1]

Hypothesis 2: *Industry has a significant impact on switching to remote work during the pandemic.*

Theoretical and empirical evidence at the enterprise level suggests that small and medium enterprises (SMEs) are more affected by the pandemic than large enterprises due to their lack of reserve capital, greater representation in industries assuming interpersonal contact, and greater dependence on local and global supply chains (Bartik et al. 2020b; Beglaryan/Shakhmuradyan 2020; Organisation for Economic Co-operation and Development 2020; Turner/Akinremi 2020). As suggested in several studies (Runyan 2006; Sullivan-Taylor/Branicki 2011; Herbane 2019), SMEs, in general, have fewer resources to plan for and respond to crises and are disproportionately affected when such events occur. Human resource management in these enterprises, like most other practices, is characterised by informality, rapid decision-making, and effective internal communications (Dundon/Wilkinson 2018). As emphasised in studies on organisational resilience, these same characteristics make SMEs more capable of adapting routines and strategies in response to exogenous shocks (Runyan 2006; Sullivan-Taylor/Branicki 2011). In other words, SMEs have the 'liability of smallness' in accessing markets and acquiring financial and human resources for dai-

---

1 In referring to professionals, we follow the definition of the United States Equal Opportunity Commission (2021) as *'occupations requiring either college graduation or experience of such kind and amount as to provide a comparable background'*.

ly operations but exhibit flexibility and resilience during crises (Eggers 2020). Based on this literature, we advance our final hypothesis as follows:

Hypothesis 3: *During the COVID-19 pandemic, small and medium enterprises have implemented remote work practices faster and to a greater extent than large enterprises.*

3. Research Design and Methodology

Data used in this paper come from a labour force survey conducted in May 2020 by the Paul Avedisian Centre for Business Research and Development (CBRD) at the American University of Armenia. The survey used a territorially stratified random sampling methodology, and the resulting sample size (n=1,312) is representative of Armenia (Centre for Business Research and Development 2020a). The questionnaire (Centre for Business Research and Development 2020b) had 22 questions, designed to obtain both demographic (age, gender, educational attainment, job classification, and monthly income) and labour market (industry of occupation, employment position, and status of employment during the pandemic) data. One of the questions measured the size of respondents' employing enterprises, enabling the classification of those as either small and medium (1–249 employees) or large (250 and more employees).[2]

The dataset used in this study has 944 observations for the *enterprise size* variable, as not all respondents answered the question on enterprise size due to being unemployed, employed as sole proprietors in industry or services, or being in agriculture. The enterprise size variable is coded in two versions: one as binary (0=large enterprises, 1=SMEs), and one as ordinal with the following categories: 1–9 employees, 10–49 employees, 50–249 employees, and 250 and more employees. Other variables in the dataset include remote work during the lockdown and immediately after it (March-April and May 2020), gender, age, residence region, education, income, industry, occupation, and managerial role. All are coded as binary, except for age, which is ordinal with three categories: 18–34, 35–54, and 55 and over (see Table 1).

---

2 Such classification is based on the *Armenian Law on State Support to Small and Medium Entrepreneurship* (adopted in 2000), which was aligned with the EU legislation in 2010 (National Assembly of the Republic of Armenia 2000; European Commission 2003).

Table 1. Variable Measurement and Coding

Variable (abbreviation)	Measurement	Coding
Enterprise size (size)	Binary	0=large enterprises
		1=SMEs
	Ordinal	1=1–9 employees
		2=10–49 employees
		3=50–249 employees
		4=250+ employees
Remote work 1 (rem1)	Binary	0=did not work remotely in March-April
		1=worked remotely in March-April
Remote work 2 (rem2)	Binary	0=did not work remotely in May
		1=worked remotely in May
Gender (gen)	Binary	0=male
		1=female
Age (age)	Ordinal	1=ages 18–34
		2=ages 35–54
		3=ages 55 and over
Residence (res)	Binary	0=marzes (Armenian regions outside capital)
		1=capital city Yerevan
Education (edu)	Binary	0=low to middle
		1=higher*
Income (inc)	Binary	0=low**
		1=middle and high
Industry (ind)	Binary	0=unable to work from home
		1=able to work from home***
Managerial role (man)	Binary	0=non-managerial
		1=managerial
Professional occupation (prof)	Binary	0=non-professionals****
		1=middle and high professionals

Notes: * bachelor's, master's, and advanced degrees. ** up to AMD 120,000 (median wage). *** based on earlier studies on the impact of the pandemic (del Rio-Chanona et al. 2020; Dingel/Neiman 2020), includes the following industries: information and communications; finance and insurance; real estate; professional, scientific, and technical services; education. **** includes clerical and administrative employees, as well as non-qualified workers in agriculture and industry.

Remote work is analysed through the following specification of a multivariate logistic regression model: *Remote work* depends on the enterprise size, age, gender, educational attainment, residence, income, job classification, and position of the employees, as well as the industry of operations. As there are two dependent variables for remote work, *worked remotely during the lockdown* (March-April 2020) and *worked remotely after the lockdown* (May 2020), there are two models to be tested, as follows:

(1) $\text{logit}[P(rem1 = 1)] = \alpha + \beta_1 size + \beta_2 gen + \beta_3 age + \beta_4 res + \beta_5 edu + \beta_6 inc + \beta_7 ind + \beta_8 man + \beta_9 prof$

(2) $\text{logit}[P(rem2 = 1)] = \alpha + \beta_1 size + \beta_2 gen + \beta_3 age + \beta_4 res + \beta_5 edu + \beta_6 inc + \beta_7 ind + \beta_8 man + \beta_9 prof$

4. Findings

Descriptive statistics of the eleven variables (see Table 2) suggest that less than a third (15.7 %) of the respondents worked remotely during the lockdown in Armenia (March-April 2020) and immediately after it in May 2020 (10 %). Over three-fourths (76.8 %) were employed by small and medium enterprises, and around half (43.5 %) were employed by enterprises having less than ten employees. The sample includes a slightly higher proportion of males (53.6 % of total) than females, and a higher proportion of residents of regions than the capital city (54.7 % and 45.3 %, respectively). Older respondents (aged 55 and over) constitute only a small fraction (4.1 %) of the sample.[3]

There are almost equal numbers of respondents with low to medium (48.3 %) and higher (51.7 %) educational attainment in the sample. Around two-thirds (64.4 %) have lower monthly income, i.e., less than or equal to the gross median wage in Armenia, AMD 120 thousand (around EUR 190 as of February 2021). The majority of respondents (79.3 %) are employed in industries where work mostly cannot be carried out remotely: agriculture, mining, manufacturing, construction, trade, transportation, food and accommodation, healthcare, arts, entertainment, and leisure. Less than 10 % of the respondents are in managerial positions, and around a third (32.2 %) are employed as professionals.[4]

---

[3] These estimates are close but not identical to official statistical data, according to which around 70 % of the employed population is employed by SMEs, males constitute 59.1 % of the employed population, and 33.5 % of the labour force is in Yerevan (Statistical Committee of the Republic of Armenia 2020a, 2020b).

[4] These estimates are also close to official statistics, according to which 31.2 % of the employed population have tertiary education, 63.8 % of the employed population is in industries where work mostly cannot be carried out remotely, 0.4 % of the employed are managers, and 20.7 % of the employed are professionals (Statistical Committee of the Republic of Armenia 2020a).

Table 2. Descriptive Statistics of the Variables

Variable	Observations	Category Breakdown
Enterprise size	944	219 (23.2 %) large enterprises
		725 (76.8 %) SMEs
		411 (43.5 %) 1–9 employees
		167 (17.7 %) 10–49 employees
		152 (16.1 %) 50–249 employees
		214 (22.7 %) 250+ employees
Remote 1	752	634 (84.3 %) commuted to workplace
		118 (15.7 %) worked remotely
Remote 2	752	677 (90.0 %) commuted to workplace
		75 (10.0 %) worked remotely
Gender	944	506 (53.6 %) males
		438 (46.4 %) females
Age	944	545 (57.7 %) ages 18–34
		361 (38.2 %) ages 35–54
		38 (4.1 %) ages 55+
Region	944	516 (54.7 %) marzes (Armenian regions outside capital)
		428 (45.3 %) capital city Yerevan
Education	944	456 (48.3 %) low to middle
		488 (51.7 %) higher
Income	944	608 (64.4 %) low
		336 (35.6 %) middle and high
Industry	944	749 (79.3 %) non-"teleworkable"
		195 (20.7 %) "teleworkable"
Managerial role	717	671 (93.6 %) non-managerial
		46 (6.4 %) managerial
Professional occupation	944	640 (67.8 %) non-professionals
		304 (32.2 %) professionals

Table 3. χ2 Test Statistics

	Size	rem1	rem2	gen	age	res	edu	inc	ind	man	prof
size		4.1** (0.05)	1.3 (0.26)	0.0 (0.94)	2.28 (0.34)	43.8*** (0.00)	19.7***(0.00)	59.9 (0.00)	51.7*** (0.00)	0.41 (0.59)	12.6*** (0.00)
rem1			329.2***(0.00)	22.6*** (0.00)	0.09 (0.97)	10.4*** (0.00)	50.5*** (0.00)	8.91*** (0.00)	78.1*** (0.00)	5.35** (0.03)	22.1*** (0.00)
rem2				17.6*** (0.00)	0.45 (0.83)	1.67 (0.22)	24.1*** (0.00)	4.08** (0.05)	39.7*** (0.00)	0.87 (0.42)	20.7*** (0.00)
gen					8.54*** (0.01)	4.08** (0.04)	20.4*** (0.00)	11.5** (0.01)	16.9*** (0.00)	0.00 (1.00)	0.17 (0.73)
age						6.52** (0.04)	1.29 (0.54)	2.94 (0.22)	0.89 (0.61)	20.1*** (0.00)	3.52 (0.18)
res							37.4*** (0.00)	78.0*** (0.00)	10.0*** (0.00)	10.7*** (0.01)	19.0*** (0.00)
edu								60.8*** (0.00)	174.9*** (0.00)	10.9*** (0.00)	81.7*** (0.00)
inc									19.9*** (0.00)	8.86*** (0.00)	37.0*** (0.00)
ind										1.43 (0.23)	122.0*** (0.00)
man											36.2*** (0.00)
prof											

Notes: ** p ≤ 0.05, *** p ≤ 0.01. Fisher's exact test statistics in parentheses.

χ^2 test statistics (see Table 3) suggest that there is statistical dependence between working from home during the lockdown *(rem1)* and all the variables, except for age. Notably, all the statistics are significant at the 1 % level, with the highest associations among being between remote work and industry (χ^2=78.1) and education (χ^2=50.5). Remote work after the lockdown *(rem2)* is statistically associated with five variables, four of which (gender, education, industry, and professional occupation) are significant at the 1 % level. The highest association is between working from home and industry (χ^2=39.7).

Logistic regression results for each of the remote work variables (see Table 4) suggest that gender, industry, and job classification have the most significant impact on working from home. Females were more than twice as likely to work from home than males both during (*OR*=2.27, *p*<0.01) and immediately after the lockdown (*OR*=2.71, *p*<0.01). Employees of industries that were coded as enabling remote work (information and communications; finance and insurance; real estate; professional, scientific, and technical services; education) were more than three times as likely to work from home during the lockdown (*OR*=3.47, *p*<0.01) and more than two times as likely to work remotely immediately after the lockdown (*OR*=2.58, *p*<0.01) than their counterparts in other industries. Individuals who are employed as professionals were more likely to work from home both during (*OR*=2.20, *p*<0.01) and after the lockdown (*OR*=3.03, *p*<0.01).

Table 4. Logistic Regression Results 1

Dependent variable	Remote Work during the Lockdown		Remote Work after the Lockdown	
Independent variables	Odds ratio	95 % confidence interval	Odds ratio	95 % confidence interval
Enterprise size	1.60 (0.46)*	(0.91; 2.82)	1.58 (0.54)	(0.80; 3.09)
Gender	2.27 (0.55)***	(1.41; 3.64)	2.71 (0.80)***	(1.52; 4.83)
Age	0.78 (0.16)	(0.52; 1.16)	0.72 (0.17)	(0.44; 1.15)
Region	1.10 (0.28)	(0.67; 1.80)	0.68 (0.21)	(0.38; 1.24)
Education	3.65 (1.42)***	(1.71; 7.80)	2.49 (1.06)**	(1.08; 5.76)
Income	1.16 (0.31)	(0.70; 1.93)	1.31 (0.40)	(0.71; 2.39)
Industry	3.47 (0.89)***	(2.10; 5.73)	2.58 (0.78)***	(1.42; 4.67)
Manager	2.82 (1.23)**	(1.20; 6.63)	2.73 (1.50)*	(0.94; 7.99)
Professional	2.20 (0.59)***	(1.30; 3.71)	3.03 (0.99)***	(1.60; 5.76)
Constant	0.01 (0.01)***	(0.01; 0.04)	0.01 (0.01)***	(0.01; 0.04)
LR χ^2 (9)	116.6***		70.1***	
Pseudo R^2	0.19		0.15	
Observations	704		704	

Notes: * p ≤ 0.10, ** p ≤ 0.05, *** p ≤ 0.01. Standard errors in parentheses.

The results also suggest that employees who have higher education were more than three times as likely to work from home during (OR=3.65, p<0.01) and more than two times as likely to work from home immediately after the lockdown (OR=2.49, p<0.05). Employees in managerial positions were around three times as likely to work from home both during the lockdown (OR=2.82, p<0.05) and after it (OR=2.73, p<0.10). Enterprise size had a significant impact on working from only during the lockdown, with SME employees being more likely to work from home (OR=1.60, p<0.10). The respondents' age, the region of residence, and income do not have a significant impact on remote work either during the lockdown or after it. Overall, the two models have a moderately good fit (pseudo-R^2=0.19 and 0.15, respectively), with significance patterns being mostly consistent during and after the lockdown.

The logistic regression results with an ordinal enterprise size variable (see Table 5) suggest that it is enterprises of medium size (having 50–249 employees), rather than micro (1–9) and small (10–49 employees) enterprises that implemented remote work practices during the lockdown (OR=2.44, p<0.01).

Table 5. Logistic Regression Results 2

Dependent variable			Remote Work during the Lockdown		Remote Work after the Lockdown	
Independent variables			Odds ratio	95 % confidence interval	Odds ratio	95 % confidence interval
Enterprise size (base: 250+)	1–9		1.08 (0.37)	(0.55; 2.13)	1.48 (0.60)	(0.67; 3.29)
	10–49		1.22 (0.43)	(0.61; 2.43)	1.15 (0.49)	(0.50; 2.63)
	50–249		2.44 (0.84)***	(1.24; 4.78)	1.84 (0.75)	(0.83; 4.10)
Gender			2.30 (0.56)***	(1.43; 3.71)	2.77 (0.82)***	(1.55; 4.95)
Age			0.77 (0.16)	(0.52; 1.16)	0.72 (0.18)	(0.45; 1.17)
Region			1.07 (0.27)	(0.65; 1.76)	0.67 (0.20)	(0.37; 1.22)
Education			3.77 (1.47)***	(1.76; 8.10)	2.57 (1.10)**	(1.11; 5.94)
Income			1.09 (0.28)	(0.65; 1.80)	1.27 (0.39)	(0.69; 2.33)
Industry			3.23 (0.84)***	(1.94; 5.36)	2.56 (0.79)***	(1.40; 4.71)
Manager			2.97 (1.30)***	(1.26; 7.02)	2.82 (1.55)	(0.96; 8.26)
Professional			2.10 (0.57)***	(1.24; 3.56)	3.02 (0.99)***	(1.58; 5.75)
Constant			0.02 (0.01)***	(0.01; 0.05)	0.01 (0.01)***	(0.00; 0.05)
LR χ^2 (11)			122.6***		70.9***	
Pseudo R^2			0.20		0.15	
Observations			704		704	

Notes: * $p \leq 0.10$, ** $p \leq 0.05$, *** $p \leq 0.01$. Standard errors in parentheses.

5. Discussion and Implications

The findings of the preceding section suggest that only a small fraction of the workforce in Armenia transitioned to remote work due to the COVID-19 pandemic, and some employees who worked from home during the lockdown went back to workplaces immediately after it was lifted in May 2020. Gender, employment as a professional, and education are all found to have a significant impact on working from home during the pandemic, with women, professionals, and employees with higher education being more likely to work from home. Employment in a managerial position has a less significant impact on remote work, suggesting that managers might have attended workplaces during and after the lockdown to keep things running. The finding for professionals supports the first hypothesis and being consistent with earlier studies (Bartik et al. 2020 a; Béland et al. 2020; Brynjolfsson et al. 2020), reflects the ability of high-wage earners to work from home.

Logistic regression results suggest that industry has the greatest impact on remote work. Similar to other studies on the impact of the pandemic (Bartik et al. 2020 a; del Rio-Chanona et al. 2020; Dingel/Neiman 2020; Saltiel 2020), it was found that workers in industries that allow for remote work, such as information and communications, finance and insurance, and education, were significantly more likely to work from home than the employees of industries assuming interpersonal contact, both during the lockdown and after it. Thus, the second hypothesis, which postulated that industry has a significant impact on remote work under the pandemic, is also supported.

It can be observed from the logistic regression results that enterprise size has a significant impact on remote work only during the lockdown (March-April), with SME employees being more likely to work from home. The breakdown of SMEs by size category (1–9, 10–49, and 50–249 employees) suggests that medium-sized (50–249 employees) but not micro and small enterprises (1–49 employees) had introduced and implemented remote work practices. Notably, there is a general consistency of the variable significance patterns during and after the lockdown models, except for the enterprise size, which suggests that small and medium enterprises resumed on-site operations as the lockdown was lifted.[5] Thus, the third hypothesis is supported only partially.

The findings of this research suggest that to build human resource management capacity for future crises of similar (healthcare-induced lockdown) nature, businesses need to allocate resources to information and communication technologies, as well as employee training aimed at digital and communication skills development. This would enable more effective and efficient transition to remote operations (Branicki/Steyer/Sullivan-Taylor 2019; Papadopoulos/Bal-

---

5 This may be attributed to the greater representation of SMEs in industries assuming interpersonal contact. See Beglaryan and Shakhmuradyan (2020) for an overview.

tas/Balta 2020). The implications for public policy reaffirm the need to invest in education, as well as technologies and infrastructures that enable remote work. For instance, the requirement to file payroll taxes electronically since the enactment of the pension reform in Armenia (2014) has helped to train accountants over the years, thus enabling a smoother transition of many professionals in the accounting field to remote work under the pandemic.

6. Conclusion

This study aimed to contribute to the literature on human resource management under the COVID-19 pandemic by examining remote work in Armenia. A representative labour force survey dataset was utilised for that purpose, and it was found that industry has the most significant impact on remote work, followed by gender and occupation of the employees. SMEs in general have implemented remote work practices faster than large enterprises, but it was medium-sized, not micro and small enterprises, that switched to remote work. More importantly, medium enterprises transitioned to remote only during the lockdown, reverting to on-site operations once it was lifted. The findings of this research are consistent with empirical evidence from other countries, suggesting that private enterprises need to invest in on-the-job training and development of the employees to build human resource management capacity for future pandemic crises.

References

Agarwal, P. (2021): Shattered but smiling: Human resource management and the wellbeing of hotel employees during COVID-19, in: *International Journal of Hospitality Management*, 93, 102765. https://doi.org/10.1016/j.ijhm.2020.102765

Bailey, K./Breslin, D. (2021): The COVID 19 pandemic: What can we learn from past research in organizations and management? in: *International Journal of Management Reviews*, 23 (1), 3–6. https://doi.org/10.1111/ijmr.12237

Bartik, A./Cullen, Z./Glaeser, E./Luca, M./Stanton, C. (2020 a): What jobs are being done at home during the COVID-19 crisis? Evidence from firm-level surveys, in: *NBER Working Paper Series*, 27422, June. https://www.nber.org/papers/w27422

Bartik, A./Bertrand, M./Cullen, Z./Glaeser, E./Luca, M./Stanton, C. (2020 b): The impact of COVID-19 on small business outcomes and expectations, in: *Proceedings of the National Academy of Sciences,* 117, 30, 17656–17666. https://doi.org/10.1073/pnas.2006991117

Beglaryan, M./Shakhmuradyan, G. (2020): The impact of COVID-19 on small and medium-sized enterprises in Armenia: Evidence from a labor force survey, in: *Small Business International Review,* 4, 2, e298. https://doi.org/10.26784/sbir.v4i2.298

Béland, L.-P./Brodeur, A./Wright, T. (2020): The short-term economic consequences of COVID-19: Exposure to disease, remote work and government response, in: *IZA Discussion Paper Series,* 13159, April. http://hdl.handle.net/10419/216471

Branicki, L./Steyer, V./Sullivan-Taylor, B. (2019): Why resilience managers aren't resilient, and what human resource management can do about it, in: *International Journal of Human Resource Management*, 30, 8, 1261–1286. https://doi.org/10.1080/09585192.2016.1244104

Brynjolfsson, E./Horton, J. H./Ozimek, A./Rock, D./Sharma, G./TuYe, H. (2020): COVID-19 and remote work: An early look at US data, in: *NBER Working Paper Series*, 27344, June. http://www.nber.org/papers/w27344

Caligiuri, P./De Cieri, H./Minbaeva, D./Verbeke, A./Zimmermann, A. (2020): International HRM insights for navigating the COVID-19 pandemic: Implications for future research and practice, in: *Journal of International Business Studies*, 51, 697–713. https://doi.org/10.1057/s41267-020-00335-9

Carnevale, J. B./Hatak, I. (2020): Employee adjustment and well-being in the era of COVID-19: Implications for human resource management, in: *Journal of Business Research*, 116, 183–187. https://doi.org/10.1016/j.jbusres.2020.05.037

Centre for Business Research and Development (CBRD) (2020 a): Employment patterns during the COVID-19 pandemic in Armenia: A brief report of labour force survey results, available at: https://cbe.aua.am/files/2020/07/CBRD_COVID19_Survey-Results_Brief-Report_ENG.pdf

Centre for Business Research and Development (CBRD) (2020 b): Working conditions during the COVID-19 pandemic in Armenia: Survey questionnaire, available at: https://cbe.aua.am/files/2020/06/COVID-19_Questionnaire_20.05.2020.pdf

del Rio-Chanona, R. M./Mealy, P./Pichler, A./Lafond, F./Farmer, D. (2020): Supply and demand shocks in the COVID-19 pandemic: An industry and occupation perspective, in: *Oxford Review of Economic Policy*, 36, S1, S94-S137. https://doi.org/10.1093/oxrep/graa033

Dingel, J. J./Neiman, B. (2020): How many jobs can be done at home? in: *Journal of Public Economics*, 189, 104235. https://doi.org/10.1016/j.jpubeco.2020.104235

Dundon, T./Wilkinson, A. (2018): HRM in small and medium-sized enterprises (SMEs), in: Collings, D. G./Wood, G. T./Szamosi, L. T. (eds.): Human resource management: A critical approach, second edition, London: Routledge, 194–211. https://doi.org/10.4324/9781315299556

Eggers, F. (2020): Masters of disasters? Challenges and opportunities for SMEs in times of crisis, in: *Journal of Business Research*, 116, 199–208. https://doi.org/10.1016/j.jbusres.2020.05.025

European Commission (2003): Commission recommendation of 6 May 2003 concerning the definition of micro, small and medium-sized enterprises, in: *Official Journal of the European Union*, L, 124, 36–41. https://eur-lex.europa.eu/eli/reco/2003/361/oj

Gabrielyan, V. (2020): COVID-19 and working from home: What are the global and local trends? *Centre for Business Research and Development Research Note Series*, July, available at: https://cbe.aua.am/files/2020/07/Gabrielyan__COVID19-and-Working-from-Home-1.pdf

Herbane, B. (2019): Rethinking organizational resilience and strategic renewal in SMEs, in: *Entrepreneurship and Regional Development*, 31, 5–6, 476–495. https://doi.org/10.1080/08985626.2018.1541594

International Labour Organisation (ILO) (2021): *COVID-19 and the world of work*, available at: https://www.ilo.org/global/topics/coronavirus/lang--en/index.htm

International Monetary Fund (IMF) (2021): *World economic outlook reports,* available at: https://www.imf.org/en/Publications/WEO

LaBerge, L./O'Toole, C./Schneider, J./Smaje, K. (2020): How COVID-19 has pushed companies over the technology tipping point—and transformed business forever. *McKinsey & Company,* October, available at: https://www.mckinsey.com/business-functions/strategy-and-corporate-finance/our-insights/how-covid-19-has-pushed-companies-over-the-technology-tipping-point-and-transformed-business-forever

National Assembly of the Republic of Armenia (2000): Law of the Republic of Armenia on state support to small and medium entrepreneurship (in Armenian, as amended December 2010), available at: https://www.arlis.am/DocumentView.aspx?DocID=64617

Organisation for Economic Co-operation and Development (OECD) (2020): *Coronavirus (COVID-19): SME policy responses,* July, available at: http://www.oecd.org/coronavirus/policy-responses/coronavirus-covid-19-sme-policy-responses-04440101/

Organisation for Economic Co-operation and Development (OECD) (2021): *Tackling coronavirus (COVID-19): Contributing to a global effort,* available at: https://www.oecd.org/coronavirus/en/

Papadopoulos, T./Baltas, K. N./Balta, M. E. (2020): The use of digital technologies by small and medium enterprises during COVID-19: Implications for theory and practice, in: *International Journal of Information Management,* 55, 102192. https://doi.org/10.1016/j.ijinfomgt.2020.102192

Runyan, R. C. (2006): Small business in the face of crisis: Identifying barriers to recovery from a natural disaster, in: *Journal of Contingencies and Crisis Management,* 14, 1, 12–26. https://doi.org/10.1111/j.1468-5973.2006.00477.x

Saltiel, F. (2020): Who can work from home in developing countries? in: Wyplosz, C. (ed.): Covid economics: Vetted and real-time papers, issue 6, London: CEPR Press, 104–118.

Statistical Committee of the Republic of Armenia (2020 a): Labour market in Armenia, 2018–2019. Yerevan. https://www.armstat.am/en/?nid=82&id=2348

Statistical Committee of the Republic of Armenia (2020 b): Small and medium entrepreneurship in the Republic of Armenia. Yerevan. https://www.armstat.am/en/?nid=82&id=2346

Sullivan-Taylor, B./Branicki, L. (2011): Creating resilient SMEs: Why one size might not fit all, in: *International Journal of Production Research,* 49, 18, 5565–5579. https://doi.org/10.1080/00207543.2011.563837

Turner, J./Akinremi, T. (2020): The business effects of pandemics – a rapid literature review, in: *ERC Insight Paper Series,* April, available at: https://www.enterpriseresearch.ac.uk/publications/the-business-effects-of-pandemics-a-rapid-literature-review/

United States Equal Opportunity Commission (2021): *Federal sector reports appendix 1: Glossary definitions,* available at: https://www.eeoc.gov/federal-sector/reports/appendix-1-glossarydefinitions

Verma, S./Gustafsson, A. (2020): Investigating the emerging COVID-19 research trends in the field of business and management: A bibliometric analysis approach, in: *Journal of Business Research,* 118, September, 253–261. https://doi.org/10.1016/j.jbusres.2020.06.057

World Bank (2021): *Global economic prospects,* available at: https://www.worldbank.org/en/publication/global-economic-prospects

World Health Organisation (2021): *Coronavirus disease (COVID-19) pandemic,* available at: https://www.who.int/emergencies/diseases/novel-coronavirus-2019